FULL CIRCLE

The very place the sole of my feet treads upon was God's gift to me.

DEBBIE DUNCAN-WHYTE

Bridgeport, CT 06605
www.hovpub.com

Full Circle
The very place the sole of my feet tread upon was God's gift to me.

HOV Publishing a division of HOV, LLC.
Bridgeport, CT 06605
Email: hopeofvision@gmail.com / www.hovpub.com

Cover Design and inside text design/layout by Hope of Vision Designs
Editor: Genesis Literary Indulgence Editing Services
Proofreaders: HOV Publishing Editorial Staff

Contact the Author: Debbie Duncan-Whyte at: debbieduncan2830@gmail.com

For further information regarding special discounts on bulk purchases, please contact:
Debbie Duncan-Whyte at debbieduncan2830@gmail.com.

ISBN Paperback: 978-1-955107-61-7
ISBN Hardcase: 978-1-955107-60-0
ISBN eBook: 978-1-955107-59-4

Printed in the United States of America

DEDICATION

I dedicate this book to my wonderful mother, Merle Cynthia Duncan. She was an extraordinary woman. Resourcefulness and selflessness were some of the qualities she mastered. From my view Merle Cynthia Duncan was an entrepreneur in Trinidad in the fifties and sixties before the word had real meaning. She raised seven children, while having limited education and resources demonstrating sheer brilliance. She had skills she didn't learn in a classroom. She did it all. I thank her for raising me, educating me, and giving me a fighting chance at life. Most importantly I thank her for guiding me to the Savior; Jesus Christ, because of her foresight I was able to not just survive but thrive. She injected the words "The battle is the LORD'S" into my vein. Merle Cynthia Duncan taught me perseverance and endurance and made me the woman I am today. Rest in Power Mammy Merle, till we meet again. I will always love you. Debbie.

Merle Cynthia Duncan, Mother

ACKNOWLEDGEMENTS

It is a true saying that it takes a village. If not for these individuals in my village I would not be here today. I want to thank Sharon Warner for extending kindness as I exit the plane. You may not know this Sharon, but it all started with your love and compassion for me at JFK airport. The sisters that lived on Church Avenue I thank you, because of you both I never was homeless. My village is filled with a vast amount of supporters and true believers and I owe it all to them. From my Transit coworkers to the wide array of customers, I say thank you. I want to thank everyone that sowed a word into my life and prayed for me through the years. I say thank you. To my friend Dorrie, you were a strong shoulder for me when Mammy Merle passed away. I say thank you. I especially want to thank Minister Eleanor Riley for encouraging me to erect an altar. My prayer life has never been the same.

I have a group of friends that span over forty years and they kept my village from going up in flames. Michelle,

Denise, Marcia, Delores, Anette, and Anita. This outstanding group of women carried me, in various seasons of my life when I was unable to do it for myself. I want to thank them for truly being my support system.

Last but not least, I want to thank my family. How do I define my family? I will say thanks to my husband and children who love me unconditionally. They never gave up on me, they loved me with all my imperfection. They supported me even when I fell short and made many mistakes. They lifted me up and motivated me in spite of all my shortcomings and flaws. Now that's my family. I am going to end with the words in Hebrew taught to me by my Jewish employer Alice, Toda Raba. Thank you.

CONTENTS

INTRODUCTION

Full Circle is about a 23-year-old Immigrant young woman leaving her family and homeland of Trinidad and Tobago in pursuit of a better life. Debbie had a deep sordid secret and feared it would soon be discovered, as she took a giant leap of faith and boarded a plane bound for the United States of America. Debbie never knew what awaited her as she strolled through the turnstiles at HOPKINSON AVENUE SUBWAY STATION; with her shoulders dropped, she embarked into the unknown. Now join her as she takes you on the ride of her life. A life plagued with heartache, pain, valleys, and many disappointments.

Read how she fought for her survival in the concrete jungle of New York City and now smiles from her mountain top. Listen as the conductor announces, "STAND CLEAR THE CLOSING DOORS" and with all the twists and turns Debbie held on and came to her destination. Imagine how gratifying it was when she came to her stop at Rockaway Avenue. Yes, they are one in the same. The very same HOPKINSON AVENUE SUBWAY STATION she exited thirty-five years ago, brought her back to that very station now called ROCKAWAY AVENUE SUBWAY STATION. Debbie worked and retired from the very same Station. It was then she realized that God was the conductor of her life. She assumed God wouldn't remember her in another country, however she was wrong. The Omnipresent God protected and shielded her from various harm and dangers and fortified her with the strength to endure all of her adversities. The Omnipresent God had a plan to give her an expected end. Debbie's life was indeed an express train ride. With God in control, Debbie Duncan's life ultimately came FULL CIRCLE.

CHAPTER 1

Walking by Faith

(Hebrew 11:1 & 6) Now faith is the substance of things hoped for, the evidence of things not seen; But without faith it is impossible to please him: for he that cometh to God must believe that he is, and that He is a rewarder of them who diligently seek him.

The plane landed at JFK international airport on October 17, 1987. I was a 23-year-old young mother of a four-year-old daughter that I sadly said goodbye to some hours earlier. I had run out of options in Trinidad, and I came to the conclusion that I needed a fresh start. The only way I was going to make it was to leave everything that was familiar behind and begin in an environment that was completely foreign. Leaving my homeland weighed heavily on my mind, however I was willing to make the sacrifice for a better life. The trip was risky, but I had to do something. I had $85 in my purse, determination in my veins and the covering of the Holy Spirit. I had the tools, and my mind was made up and I was going to make my move. My goal in my heart was simple. I was going to America to make a better life for myself and my young daughter Latonya.

> *(Joshua 1:9) Have I not commanded thee? Be strong and of good courage; be not afraid, neither be thou dismayed; for the LORD thy God is with thee whithersoever thou goest.*

I had every intention of returning to Trinidad for my daughter. I just didn't want to jeopardize her safety by taking her on this journey. There were just too many unknowns that loomed ahead. As desperate as I was to leave Trinidad, I wholeheartedly wanted my daughter to leave with me. However, I knew I couldn't subject her to the uncertainty. I was counting on my mother Merle Cynthia Duncan, known to all as (Mammy Merle) to help me carry out my plan. My mother knew God and worshiped *Him* faithfully. My mother was the person who initially introduced me to God. Daily Mammy Merle would testify of God's goodness and *His* faithfulness towards her. I understand now that God really speaks to the heart of *His* people. God spoke to my mother's heart, and she agreed to take care of Latonya.

> *(Proverbs 21:1) The king's heart is in the hand of the LORD, as the rivers of water: he turneth it withersoever he will.*

My beloved mother was the anchor that held everyone down, so her support was significant. Her confidence in me and encouraging words helped calm my anxiety. With her reassurance and support I had a sense of peace. We both knew that the stakes were high traveling to America. I wasn't sure of my living arrangements. I literally was stepping out on faith. My mother also was fully aware of the dangers and challenges. Most of her friends were living in America, and they informed her of the difficulties that loomed ahead. After a long and drawn-out discussion we both agreed it was wise to leave Latonya behind. In her care Latonya would receive the naturing every child needs at that tender age. There was no one more suitable than my mother to care for her. Deep in my heart the decision just felt right. All my life I witnessed my mother's tenacity and strength. If I had an ounce of that in my vein, I knew I was going to make it in America and one day return for my daughter Latonya.

I was removing fear and uncertainty and placing everything in God's hands. I was determined to find my way. Since childhood I have witnessed God taking care of my mother. My mother was passionate and committed when it came to her love of the Lord. She vehemently relied on *His* strength, and *He* never failed her. She boasted daily of *His* faithfulness and her confidence in *Him* and *His* word. She testified and genuinely believed in the promises of God. I assumed if I followed everything my mother did: loved, worshiped, and praised God I would be fine. God knew my mother and she knew *Him*. Now as for me, God knew me from my mother's womb, but the question is, did I know *God*? I am unbuckling my seatbelt, and I'm about to find out.

(Acts 16:31) And they said, Believe on the Lord Jesus Christ, and thou shalt be saved, and thy house.

I made my way to the customs officer, and my visa was scrutinized from top to bottom. One more minute standing there and I would have passed out. I was so nervous. I am finally cleared to enter the United States. Thank God my secret is undetected. I just have to make it through those glass doors, and I am home free. I hurriedly made my way outside while my knees were buckling. I can't believe I made it. Give God Glory.

There was a slight chill in the air, something I have never felt before in my life. Little did I know this would be my very first touch of what Americans call fall. I walked outside to the receptive hugs and smiles from my dear friend Sharon and her father Mr. Warner. We walked and talked as we made our way to the bus that would connect us to the subway. It was great to see my friend. Allow me to take a moment to elaborate. Sharon was an amazing friend and also Latonya's Godmother. Sharon migrated to the United States a couple years earlier.

She lived with her father and his mother in Brooklyn. We talked about her goddaughter Latonya and what it was like leaving her behind. I was emotional just talking about it. Sharon changed the mood and inquired about her own family in Trinidad. We headed to the subways. Yes, the infamous New York City subways. There was no taxi waiting for me and neither Sharon nor her father owned a car. Honestly, I was just happy to be picked up. It really didn't matter the means or method. We made our way to the transportation that was available. Could you believe it, my very first time in the United States of America, I stepped off the plane and onto a shuttle bus to the A-Train. God, you really ordered my footsteps.

The ride on the A train from the airport was a long one. I had enough time to reveal my dilemma to Sharon, but for some reason I just could not tell her. The time was not appropriate for me to lay something that heavy on her. This situation if not handled gently had the potential to go bad very quickly and I was not ready for the seriousness of it. So, I decided to wait. We got off the train at Hopkinson Avenue; currently known as Rockaway Avenue Station. Hold onto your token, the story gets better. That is the very same

Rockaway Avenue Station that I'm currently working at 34 years later. God did say he will make a way in the wilderness.

(Jeremiah 29:11) For I know the thoughts that I think towards you, saith the Lord, thoughts of peace, and not of evil, to give you an expected end.

As we left the train station the chill intensified. I can feel the chills through my light summer dress. Happily, one block away was Sharon's home, 59 Hull Street. As I entered the house a sense of relief came over me. I genuinely thanked Sharon for coming to the airport for me. As I previously mentioned, she was a real good friend. Back home you heard stories of people being stranded at airports or family members not answering their phone calls. Thank God this was not the case. Mr. Warner brought in my one bag, no luggage. I had carry-on luggage, however only I could carry it. My blue canvas bag was stuffed with a few pieces of clothing and my precious brown candle. I knew when my mother gave me the candle it meant I had to be in constant prayer for what lay ahead. As a child we lived across the street from the well-known OUR LADY OF LAVENTILLE CATHOLIC CHURCH, so I was no stranger to prayer. I made my first communion there, went to confession and never missed *The FATIMA PROCESSION* held at the church. My mother knew I was heading into the unknown and her intuition told her only prayer to The Most High God would keep me safe. She said the brown candle which symbolized Saint Anthony wouldn't hurt because I needed all the help I could get. I kept my brown candle close and prayed daily just as advised.

> *(Psalm 18:28) For thou wilt light my candle; the Lord my God will enlighten my darkness.*

We made our way up the stairs to the second floor of the house, and I settled in for my first night's sleep at 59 Hull Street. I said a prayer for my family and also thanked God for landing the plane safely. I then closed my eyes and fell off to sleep.

> *(Psalms 3:5) I laid me down and slept; I awaked; for the LORD sustained me.*

The next morning, I met Sharon's grandmother, Mr. Warner's mother. She was a petite and soft spoken elderly woman. However, as I got closer to her that very moment the secret was out. What Sharon and her father failed to detect was immediately uncovered by old lady Warner. I had another piece of luggage "A carry on". Old lady Warner could work for the modern day TSA. In two seconds, this keen eyed senior citizen figured out what customs and border patrol missed. I WAS PREGNANT. The secret was out. I was almost six and a half months pregnant. Yes, the carry-on luggage was indeed a nicely un-noticeable baby bump. To Sharon's credit she had not seen me in years, and my stomach was quite small back then. The light summer dress also worked to my advantage. You had to look at me real close to notice I was pregnant. Sharon's grandmother did not throw me out of the house thank God, but she did voice her concerns. Her heartfelt words to me that day made me more determined to not just survive but thrive in the United States of America. Mrs. Warner eloquently stated that I will not make it in America with a baby, plain and simple. I truly believed she was not being hurtful or malicious. However, I have come to realize years later this woman was preparing me for the harsh realities of life as a young, pregnant, immigrant woman in America. I am grateful that she was direct and honest. Even if her words scared me at the time, I was not going to be deterred. I had too much at stake. There was no turning back for me.

> *(2 Timothy 1:7) For God hath not given us the spirit of fear; but of power, and of love, and of a sound mind.*

Explaining the dilemma to Sharon was not going to be easy. This was too much for anyone to absorb, however I had to try. I had to come clean and tell Sharon the truth. I sincerely explained to her that I was scared and wanted a way out. For some reason Sharon listened and she seemed to understand. I honestly wanted to tell her about the pregnancy in person. If I was going to be judged, I preferred it to be by her. I couldn't tell her on the phone I was pregnant and planning to come to America. We both knew what was going to be the outcome of that phone conversation. Sharon Warner showed me what true and genuine friendship really is. She persuaded her grandmother that I would be ok, and I had a godmother named Yvonne who was picking me up in a few days. That scenario bought me the three best nights of sleep I was blessed to have in my early days in America. As long as I live, I will never forget what Sharon did for me. Her compassion and kindness cannot be compensated. If you really want to know the truth, Sharon's help and support was the beginning of my journey. Here was another example of God talking to the heart of *His* people. I thank Sharon's grandmother for sheltering me in that season of my life in America. May her soul rest In Peace.

Fifty-Nine Hull Street was the first leg of the marathon race which is my life. I was determined and committed to run this race with God's guidance and grace. I knew when God is running with you, you run to win. Can you believe that years later the very place I started in 1987 as a scared and pregnant young immigrant woman, would be the place I call home just one block away. Once God is in the lead, I just had to remain in the race, stay the course so I can obtain the prize. To God be the Glory!

> *(1 Corinthian 9:24) Know ye not that they which run in a race run all, but one receiveth the prize? So run, that you may obtain.*

The weekend came and auntie Yvonne kept her word. We spoke on the phone and made the necessary arrangements for us to meet. I traveled by bus to her apartment and met up with her. I had to learn the transport system very quickly. I wrote everything down and made a mental note of my surroundings. As I arrived at Auntie Yvonne's apartment, she was just arriving home from her babysitting job and was happy to see me. Once we got into her apartment on Ocean Avenue, I immediately told her about the pregnancy. I just wanted to leave my cards on the table. No more secrets. The biggest hurdle was telling Sharon the truth and I had survived that. Auntie Yvonne was shocked that I took the chance and traveled to America being that far along in the pregnancy.

I recalled telling her that desperate times call for desperate measures. She said she already had a job lined up for me, but with my news we both knew no one will hire me now. She called one of her girlfriends whose name was Phyllis. Fortunately for me she had two nieces that were desperately in need of someone to babysit their young children. The arrangement was straightforward. I will take care of their kids and they will provide room and board. They promised to pay me what little they could. I went along with the deal because at this point what other option did I have.

There was no time for negotiating. I am almost six and a half months pregnant with no other family in the United States and winter is approaching. It would have been a disaster if I refused their offer. I was grateful I was not going to a shelter or even worse, on the streets.

> *(Psalm 18:32) It is God that girdeth me with strength, and maketh my way perfect.*

Photo Gallery

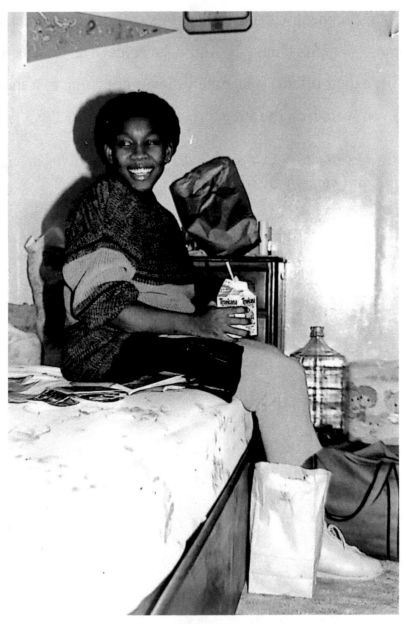

First day in New York with blue bag.

CHAPTER 2

Ocean Avenue

I am headed to 591 Ocean Avenue. I am babysitting three small children for a place to call home. I felt extremely blessed. Winter was approaching and I had secured a warm place to stay. Sandy and Suzy were the sisters that gave me my very first babysitting job. They both had mediocre jobs and were trying to survive themselves. They were struggling to raise their own small children in a studio apartment. The arrangement was not perfect to say the least, these young women were strangers to me, and yet they agreed to take me in. They were desperate and so was I. We were going to make it work as awkward as it was. I know when to be thankful. Can you imagine if these women, who were experiencing hardship of their own, did not show compassion towards me? I might've ended up on the roadside, or in a shelter in the beginning of winter. Without a doubt I can credit these young women for me never being homeless in the United States of America. I Give God Glory.

> *(Psalm 31:14) But I trusted in thee, O LORD: I said, Thou art my God.*

> *(Psalm 126:3) The LORD hath done great things for us; whereof we are glad.*

On the way home from work one day Suzy found a couch and brought it into the apartment. Someone discarded their old couch and Suzy decided that it would be great as my bed. I didn't refuse, at least it was a step up from the floor. Bringing home the couch was just a way of showing compassion. This gesture showed me that these sisters were sympathetic to my current sleeping arrangements and did something about it. When the doors opened to the apartment, you saw the couch, my new bed in the hallway. It was comforting to know that they cared, and it made me feel appreciated. These women, who weren't even family, cared about me and my wellbeing and that was gratifying. I am forever indebted to those sisters for their compassion in that trying and fragile season of my life. Bobby's Department store was around the corner, so I bought a large but cheap blanket, which served as a covering for my new bed. Never in my mind did I think of bed bugs, not one sleepless night. I am thinking that in the 80s bed bugs were not around. Thank God for that. Sleeping on a couch that was found on the street corner was seen as a step up for some and rite of passage for others. There was no shame in my game. I must say those days were rough, but from my perspective I was blessed. Pregnant with not much cash and in a foreign land I must confess God had to be with me. The 80s was the crack cocaine era, realistically I was more focused on remaining drug free and alive. Bed bugs were something you didn't think about back then. As the Rapper Jay-Z would say, "I have 99 problems" and bed bugs ain't one. I thank God because I never had one bite. God was my stay. He kept me covered.

(Psalm 121:8) The LORD shall preserve thy going out and thy coming in from this time forth, and even for evermore.

Thanksgiving came, I am two months into the fall season. The cold temperature was new and different to me. I stayed inside and kept a low profile. Thanksgiving was very different from the Thanksgiving that I grew up knowing. In Trinidad Thanksgiving would be a prayer ceremony given by anyone. The individual would be giving thanks for just about anything. They would usually invite the neighborhood children and would feed them and all the partakers. There was no shortage of food when you attended a Spiritual Baptist Thanksgiving. The preacher officiating the service would lead the partakers in prayer and singing of hymns. He would then break out in the well-known hymn; "Break bread and rejoice and rejoice in Jesus name". Everyone joined in the singing. You knew it was time to eat. As I said, there was no shortage of food. You had treats to take home in that infamous greasy brown bag. This was just one of my fondest memories growing up as a child in Trinidad. This Thanksgiving celebration was new and very different for me. How do I cope

18

with new and different things? I adapt. Christmas came and this holiday was close to what I knew and loved. I didn't have much money, but I managed to pack a box and send it to Trinidad. Everyone got something, no matter how little it was, I was able to give. This uplifted my spirits. It's exactly what Christmas was all about. Finding a way to give to my family with the little I had. It was humbling. It made me feel useful and that made me happy. Back home we were raised with little, however we were never without. My mother worked miracles, so we never experienced lack. What little money that my father gave her she would stretch it and maintain the home. We always had ham and most times a turkey for Christmas. If you didn't have a ham for Christmas, it was not Christmas. The festivities before the big day were amazing. Lots of cooking and baking. Fruit cakes and sweetbreads were my mother's specialties. We were jumping for joy when our mother announced she would be ordering Pastelle, another holiday delicacy.

Homemade bread and other baked treats were the aroma in every household in the neighborhood. We had new curtains, new sheets on the bed, new furniture and if you couldn't afford new furniture the old ones were reupholstered. The children were often blessed with new clothes and sometimes you may be treated with a toy. We traditionally would paint everything in sight. The house, the gate, the flowerpots, and the stones leading to the gate; everything had to look new because it was Christmas. As a child I often thought that Jesus was about to be born so the place had to be cleaned. The way our mother had us cleaning you would think that Jesus was being delivered in our house. When I think about it, everyone in the neighborhood must have thought Jesus was being born in their homes. Everything had to be perfect. The dishes that no one could use had to be carefully washed and pray you didn't break one item. These were precious pieces to my mother. They were irreplaceable. These pieces were intricately placed in the infamous (*buffet*). The floors had to be polished by hand. Christmas Day was very special to me as a child growing up in Trinidad. It always brings a smile to my face when I reflect on those wonderful childhood memories.

This was the first Christmas away from Latonya and it was going to be hard. I knew she would be happy with her presents. I just hope it would take away the pain of me not being there. I was missing her, and I couldn't imagine how it was for her. Sending the box kept me occupied and minimized the loneliness. God knew my heart, and *He* knew my capability. *He* is the all knowing God and *He* knew it was the best I could do with the little funds that I had. *He* was really the God of all sufficiency. God stretched what I sent for my family right before my eyes.

(Philippians 4:19) But my God shall supply all your need according to his riches in glory by Christ Jesus.

I thank God that my first Christmas in America I wasn't alone. The living arrangements with the sisters weren't perfect, however I was content. I had no regrets going to live with them. Looking back, I must say it was a horrifying state to be in. Here I am pregnant, no baby daddy around, and no money. Only God knew how I survived. I thank God for what I had and what *He* had blessed me with. I knew I had to be patient just like Mammy Merle instructed.

(Philippians 4:11-12) Not that I speak in respect of want: for I have learned, in whatsoever state I am, therewith to be content; I know how to be abased, and I

know how to abound: everywhere and in all things, I am instructed both to be full and to be hungry, both to abound and to suffer need.

I decided to call the baby's father, Sherman Superville and tell him the situation, hoping he would help. He said the only help he could offer at the time was to try and visit Latonya and enquire about her. He promised to report back to me on how she was coping. Financially he was on the same ship as me, sinking. He also had a secret. He was trying to get out of Trinidad by way of Canada. He didn't want to disclose much information because of fear of worrying me. We both were badly off just in different countries. We were both struggling and trying to find solutions and ways to adjust. Only God could help us.

(Psalm 17:5-6) Hold up my goings in thy paths, that my footsteps slip not. I have called upon thee, for thou wilt hear me, O God: incline thine ear unto me, and hear my speech.

PHOTO GALLERY

My new life in the United States (Church Avenue).

CHAPTER 3

GI Joe

The new year is here, it's January 1988 and bitter cold. My winter gear was a pink jacket to match my pink boots. I bought the jacket from Bobby's Department store, where else. That really was my everything store. I will have to ride out the winter with that pink outfit, it's all I could afford. It was fairly cheap, and I had to save every dollar from my babysitting salary for my baby that was on the way. I checked my money after the shopping spree, and I had ninety dollars left. Now I am limiting my spending to just necessities. I had not much of an appetite, so I am now rail thin. All I wanted to eat was macaroni and cheese that cost $.25 cents a box and magnesia.

I have never been to a prenatal clinic or seen a doctor since I landed, and it's now January. God help me and my unborn baby. The ninety dollars was to shop for the baby and send a few dollars to my mother for Latonya. I dare not use it for a doctor's visit. I would have to pray to God that all goes well with me and the pregnancy.

As the days went on all I wanted to eat was ice, I could not believe this, as bitter cold as it was outside, I am craving ice. One night after an ice binge the unfortunate tragedy happened. I was lying on my back, and I felt the couch was a little damp. I thought I had spilled the ice water, so I turned on the light, to my disbelief the couch was covered in blood. I could not believe it. There was so much blood I was terrified. I called out to the sisters, and they decided to send me to the hospital in a taxi. The closest Hospital was Kings County Hospital. I was so fearful. I could only rely on God's help to get to the hospital. I just needed *Him* to look my way. I don't know how I survived from losing all that blood, but God had to be with me. The doctors at the hospital said I had lost too much blood and they were going to operate. The baby was going to be delivered by C-section. There was no time, no family to call. There wasn't anyone to make medical decisions or to hold my hand. I just had to trust God and believe in *His* promises to always protect me. I remembered I signed a clipboard for the blood transfusion. I guess my blood was all left on the couch. I recall asking God to give me another chance at life and to save my baby.

When the ordeal was over, and I came out of surgery I opened my eyes. Yes, I was alive. God saved my life. I got two blood transfusions and I survived. I am alive, stitched up and in a tremendous amount of pain, but thank God I am alive. My baby also pulled through. I delivered a baby boy, weighing one pound thirteen ounces. Could you imagine a baby that small surviving? God saved my baby's life there is no question about that. The nurses said he was in the Neonatal Intensive Care Unit because there were some complications. The nurse also told me I will see him as soon as I was able to get off the bed.

Now getting off the bed was not going to be easy with eighteen stitches in my stomach. I needed to call my mother and notify her of my situation. There was no cell phone back then or at least I didn't know of anyone who owned one. So, I could not call anyone. The pain was excruciating. If you have ever had surgery in the stomach, you would know you can't even sneeze or cough without tears falling from your eyes. I think it was by day two I was able to crawl out of the bed. With the help of the IV pole, I made the walk to the NICU. When I saw my son for the first time I cried uncontrollably because he was very sick. He had tubes coming out of all areas of his body. He was so small I could not believe it. The nurse said his lungs were not quite developed. I could only look at him, but I could not hold him. He was in an incubator. It was heartbreaking. The fact that I never had prenatal care, and the lack of a daily nutritious meal contributed to his poor health. All I can think of is that God is going to help me. I crawled back to bed and cried unto the Lord. I went to God in prayer and in pain.

(Psalm 55:16) As for me, I will call upon God; and the LORD shall save me.

I cried out to him because I remembered he was a present help in the time of trouble. The nurse said they were taking good care of him, and I had to work on trying to walk. I couldn't even get to the bathroom without discomfort, and they are telling me to try to walk. I remembered delivering Latonya in Port-of-Spain General Hospital in Trinidad and it was nothing like this. I recalled a spontaneous delivery, and I was walking around the next day. A C-section is indescribable pain. I was discharged from the hospital within four days whether I was able to walk or not. If there is a silver lining to this situation, it's that the baby is going to remain in the NICU, and he will get the care that he needs. I could not take care of a baby in that condition in the heart of winter, not to mention my own physical limitations. He had no clothes, no place to sleep. What was I going to do? I couldn't take my newborn son to that bloody couch. I left the hospital distraught that he was so ill, but thankful that God kept him alive, and he could receive the proper medical care that he needed.

(1 Thessalonians 5:18) In everything give thanks: for this is the will of God in Christ Jesus concerning you.

I was experiencing some serious emotions, but I had no time to entertain them. Postpartum depression had to take a backseat to all the other problems I was facing. There was no time for me to feel sorry for myself. I had to get to a phone and call my mother. She will know what to do. I made it back to the apartment and got hold of my mother. I carefully explained the situation to her. My mother was my rock. When it came to prayers, my mother was a warrior. She said she was going into deep prayer for my son. She instructed me to call upon God with the brown candle she gave me. I relied on my mother for strength and wisdom and was confident in God for a miracle. I prayed, I begged, and bargained with God. I remembered that night praying and literally telling God if he saves my boy, I will give him the name Anthony. That night I was relentless.

(Psalm 55:17) Evening, and morning, and at noon, will I pray, and cry aloud: and he shall hear my voice.

(Psalm 102:1-2) Hear my prayer, O LORD, and let my cry come unto thee; Hide not thy face from me in the day when I am in trouble; incline thine ear unto me: in the day when I called answer me speedily.

The Lord indeed answers prayer, my son Anthony stayed in the Neonatal Intensive Care Unit for weeks. I kept my word and God kept my son alive. Every day sometimes three times a day I will go to the NICU. I had to suit up and try to feed him with a small tube. When he became a little stronger, I was encouraged by the nurses to breast-feed him. This boy was indeed a survivor. He was a fighter and he fought to live. God alone knew his path and his destiny, this almost two-pound baby would one day grow to be a real-life soldier. Could you imagine that. Anthony Duncan nineteen years later would enlist and be deployed to active duty in the war zone of Afghanistan. He served and risked his life for his country. My premature baby boy returned home alive again, and in one piece. Anthony Duncan, my soldier, was awarded a Purple Heart Medal. God saved my son for a purpose. This was no doubt my very first miracle.

(Psalm 34:4) I sought the LORD, and he heard me, and delivered me from all my fears.

The sisters back at Ocean Avenue introduced me to their cousin Debby. They said that she would be helpful because she lived close to the hospital. Debby allowed me to stay at her apartment in the daytime, so I could be with the baby at the hospital without traveling back-and-forth in the cold and the snow. Debby's arrangement worked well to my advantage. I was able to spend more time at the hospital with the baby and worry less about transportation and the bitter cold. My mother insisted that I continue to breastfeed Anthony as often as I could. She said it will help with his health and growth. I was just happy to breast-feed, just to feel him close. I was healing and so was Anthony. It took a couple more weeks to get to his discharge weight of 5 pounds. I was able to muster up some clothes and blankets from my $90 savings. The sisters chipped in and purchased a bassinet, so Anthony had a warm bed. The couch was cleaned up and a new blanket placed over it. My area in the hallway was now ready. My miracle baby was coming home. I could now proudly say that my son's life and my life was saved by the well-trained staff at KINGS COUNTY HOSPITAL. I will never forget how they worked hard to save us. I will refer anyone to what I call (LIFE SAVING KINGS COUNTY HOSPITAL). Give God Glory.

Things were now starting to come together for Sherman, he was able to hustle up some cash and when the time was right, he was going to make his big getaway. I was nervous because everything was so hush-hush. We shared the same sentiment, he couldn't be here for the birth of his son, but somehow, he was going to be here to help raise him. Things would be better for us. We will be a family. Two weeks later my hopes and dreams of Sherman joining us went up in smoke, because the deal in Canada fell through. Here I thought we were making strides and we ran into another obstacle. It would be a couple more months later that Sherman would catch a break. The break came by way of the famous Steel Pan Band, Witco Desperado. The band was going on tour and was making a stop in the United States. Sherman made it into the United States. Give God Glory.

The details were still sketchy, but I didn't need details, I needed help. The plan was that he would stay at his aunt's house in Bedford Stuyvesant, and I will remain at Ocean Avenue with the baby until we can get things organized. Anthony was growing fast. I am happy I took my mother's advice and continued breastfeeding him, no one believed he was born premature. We decided to have Anthony Christen immediately. The Church was Saint Anthony's Baptiste Church on Utica Avenue. Tony and Marcia Pierre were the Godparents. Tony was Sherman's cousin and he and his wife helped with the Christening arrangements. After the service there was a small celebration at their house. They were very supportive, and I couldn't have made it through those first couple of weeks without that couple.

That same night we made quick plans to get the baby to my mother in Trinidad. Tony fortunately for us was making plans to visit Trinidad and he agreed to take Anthony to my mother. All we needed to do was organize his birth certificate and he was set. No expense of a plane ticket and he was on his way to be with my mother and his sister. The day he was leaving was very emotional for me. Here I am, separating from another young child again. The best I could do to ease my sadness was to breast-feed him all the way to the airport. With pain in my heart, I turned over my 6-month-old son to Tony Pierre in JFK International Airport. That was the last time Sherman and I saw Anthony as an infant.

That form of separation could break any parent's heart. The only gratification was, Anthony would be with my mother and his sister Latonya.

Returning from the airport was challenging, I was experiencing every kind of emotion. Separation, frustration, heartbreak, you name it. I was an emotional wreck. How can I give birth to two children, and my mother have to raise them. I was determined that I am going to get my children and raise them myself. Returning to Trinidad one day for my children was the driving force that kept me going. My mother called and said Anthony landed safely. She reassured me that he would be fine. If there was any consolation to my sad situation, my two children were together. My dear mother was taking care of my children and reuniting with them was priority number one. Sherman and I were both undocumented, neither of us could assist the other. In moving forward, we had to have a plan in motion with no room for error. Sherman would return to his aunt's house, try to find employment, and figure out how to become legal, while staying out of the claws of immigration. It was a daunting task for Sherman, but he had to figure out a way. On the other hand, I had to find a job in someone's kitchen and stay there. Our goals were set, and we were ready. Let the hunt begin. I asked God to protect us as we maneuver the streets of Brooklyn.

(Psalm 17: 8) Keep me as the apple of the eye, hide me under the shadow of thy wings.

The year was 1988, midsummer. I called my Godmother and as always, she came through for me again. She made it clear once I was in a live-in job, I would be safe from immigration. Things didn't go like I thought. I was changing jobs every other week. Back then in the 80s you could jump from job to job. It was that easy, no hassle. Housekeepers and babysitters were in great demand. My Godmother wasn't too happy, but I couldn't adjust. I had to confess to her my feelings of loneliness and isolation. Worst of all, I desperately missed my children. She reassured me that I will be with them again once I remain focused and work hard. My Godmother made the job seem feasible, but as a twenty-three-year-old I wasn't mentally ready to be locked away in anyone's kitchen.

When I think back to all the jobs I changed, I am shocked at my rebelliousness. I just couldn't understand why a young woman who was well educated, had to clean someone's house. I couldn't comprehend the immigrant way of life. I knew I was capable of more, and it was not a mop and broom. These families didn't know that I attended private school and I had dreams and aspirations of raising my children and having my own family. I knew I had to make sacrifices, but this was just too hard. I resented the kitchen because I knew deep down in my heart God had more for me. Thanks to my abrasive God mother and her consistent reminder of my responsibilities to my children, I eventually came to my senses.

I remembered my mom telling me the bible story of how Joseph persevered in the pit and prison before prospering in the palace. I guess this was my Joseph journey. I did have my own dreams of making my way out of the kitchen. Somehow, I had to be excellent in the kitchen, and like Joseph God will eventually elevate me.

I came to understand even with my education, there were steps to success. Essentially this kitchen was going to be the catalyst to reunite me with my children. Although I knew I wasn't kitchen material, I made the ultimate sacrifice to be the best housekeeper/ babysitter that I could be. Daily my heart ached for my children and Sherman, but I knew I had to see this through. It was time for me to wake up from my dream. The family I finally settled down with was the Sterns. They were a fairly young couple with 3 children and a huge 5-bedroom house. They were nice and really down to earth. I couldn't say what it was about this particular couple, but they were just different. I thank God for placing me with the right family. I decided to put my whole heart into this job and be dedicated to the Sterns. I had to suppress all my feelings and pent up emotions and simply adjust. The Sterns hired me to clean their house and care for their children. I agreed to do the job to the best of my ability.

I was grateful that this couple was patient and also kind. With their patience and my private school reading ability, I became proficient in reading all their Jewish recipes. I quickly grew into the job. I knew there were other babysitters who weren't as fortunate as I was. I thank God for showing me favor and strength daily. As the months passed, I will occasionally whine to my Godmother about my current situation. Clearly irritated, she will always shrug it off and remind me that it was not about me. That was the way of life for an immigrant, whether you attended private school or not. I refuse to accept that as my new way of life. She made it clear that there were numerous ways for me to make money. However, this was the safest and most honest without having a green card.

I am glad I took her strict advice and stayed in the Stern's kitchen. I credit my Godmother for keeping me from unraveling. She persuaded me that in order to get my green card I had to focus and remain strong. Sadly, I began to accept the fact that I had to sacrifice my youth in the Stern's kitchen, to hold my children again and reunite with Sherman. The sad fact was I wasn't the only one that attended private school. Most housekeepers and babysitters had some type of education. However, once you arrive in America you have to be in the shadows for fear of arrest and deportation. You had to get legal documents to make your way out of the kitchen and with God's favor to the palace. Praise and thanks to God for maturing me while I was under such enormous pressure, because I remained focused and stayed in the Stern's kitchen.

I was preparing gefilte fish, carrot kugel, potato kugel and their favorite, honey lemon chicken for Sabbath. That was my life every Friday. At 9:00 am all the recipes were on the kitchen counter, and I began the cooking session. As a 23-year-old I soon found out education meant nothing when you don't have legal documents. Every Friday while cooking I knew this sacrifice was not about me and my feelings. It was simply about the welfare of my two young children.

The irony of this situation was, the Sterns had a son the same exact age as my son Anthony and their daughter was also close in age with Latonya. Imagine that! I could not nurture and raise my own son and daughter, and now I had to do it for someone else's children. Here come the emotions all over again. Anyone else would need therapy for all the emotional and physiological stress that I am under, however right now therapy will have to wait. I needed every penny for my green card. I will seek therapeutic help at a later time. God knows I needed it. There was a lot of pain inside for my children, not to mention me and Sherman growing further and further apart. We both agreed by any means necessary, but it was easier said than done. I was struggling. I could hardly see him, there was no way for us to communicate, it was just a horrible state of events. I buried myself in laundry and remained focused.

I knew working with this family was the only way to reunite with them, so I had to wait and pray for God to give us a breakthrough. The horrifying fact was, my visa has expired, and I am an undocumented immigrant, this was very unnerving to say the least. I would have to be a housekeeper for a number of years. This was a hard pill to swallow, and very scary, however I was desperate to hold my children again. I needed God's strength to persevere. I remembered my mother's words when I was leaving Trinidad that still resonates with me. Mammy Merle said in life I would have to make some hard decisions and working in the Stern's kitchen was one of them. I asked God to make this difficult situation bearable.

(Psalm 16:8) I have set the LORD always before me: because he is at my right hand, I shall not be moved.

The good news was the Stern's were young, modern and kindhearted. There was a free-spirited way about them that I couldn't explain. I just knew I felt safe with them. I was skeptical about turning over my passport to anyone but there was something special about them. Immigration was always in the back of my mind. The stories housekeepers will tell were scary. They claimed immigration will pick you up off the streets, lock you up for months and then you will be deported back to your country. Imagine if they made a sweep of the Long Island Railroad, the entire train would be empty. Back in the 80s no one had documents. For the entire train of housekeepers and babysitters there was always a high level of fear, risk, and uncertainty. Everyone had their various reasons for taking those risks. For most of us fear went out the window and perseverance and determination stepped in. We rode those trains and cleaned those houses trusting and believing in God's love and protection towards us.

(Psalm 52:8) But I am like a green olive tree in the house of God: I trust in the mercy of God for ever and ever.

(Psalm 54:.4) Behold, God is my helper: the Lord is with them that uphold my soul.

PHOTO GALLERY

Shopping at
Bobby's
Department Store
for the baby.

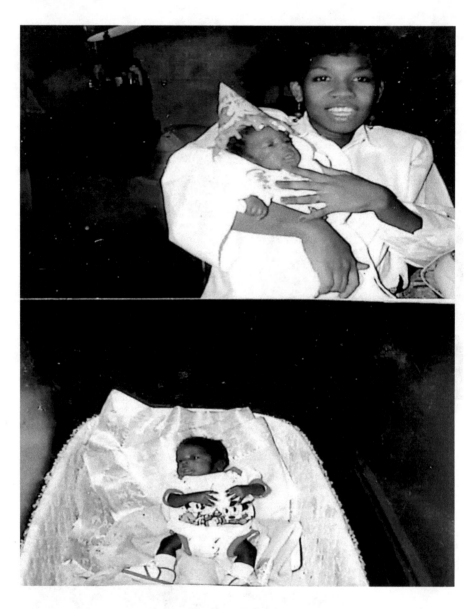

Baby Anthony discharged and going home from the
hospital at 5 lbs.

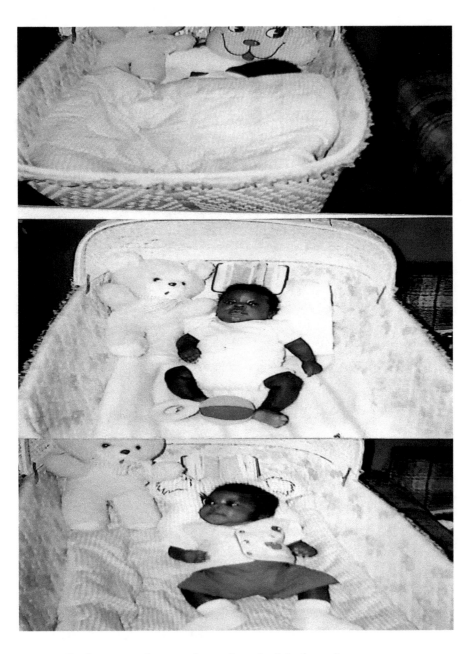

Baby growing and resting in his bassinet next to
my bed; The Brown Couch.

Baby Christening with Marcie Pierre his Godmother;
heading back to Trinidad.

My son is a real life soldier 19 years later.

CHAPTER 4

The Green Card

The year is 1989, Anthony is approaching his first birthday. It's been almost six months that I have been working for the Stern's and there is no word concerning my green card. In the meantime, Sherman was doing odd jobs with his cousin Tony, he also was desperate and anxious for his legal documents. He was thinking along the lines of marrying someone for his green card. We knew we would have to go our separate ways to make it happen. For him there weren't too many options, and we were becoming frustrated. So, we both decided that the only way to be together was to split up and pray that God leads us back to each other. I had to walk away from my baby's father and our relationship. After we fought so hard to be together, we had to say goodbye. I am twenty-three years old, and I am struggling to figure out how to endure the collapse of my relationship right before my eyes. Father God, please give me the strength and courage to move forward. My mind is being flooded with emotions. God, where are you?

> *(Psalm 66:17) I cried unto him with my mouth, and he was extolled with my tongue.*

I was becoming depressed as I saw everything slipping away from me. It was time for Anthony to get back to the United States. He had to return for his doctor's appointment, and I was not going to take any chances with the doctors. I remembered what transpired when I didn't visit a doctor and I was not going to let this happen with my son. I also found out about a studio apartment that was quite cheap. I was very excited to see it. I had to find a way to tell the Stern's what was happening and remain employed. Anthony needed his immunization shots, a physical checkup and then returned to Trinidad to be with my mother. It was a tall order that would take a lot of maneuvering, but it had to be done. Once I explained my dilemma to the Stern's they were more than happy to give me the time off. I assumed because they had a son the same age, they were sympathetic to my plight. One of my friends agreed to cover for the two weeks and it was agreed upon by the Sterns.

I left eager to hold my son once again and make a quick stop to check out the studio apartment. I had a few days before Anthony arrived and I wanted everything perfect for him. I saw the apartment and signed the lease on the spot. Look at me, my very own apartment. It wasn't luxurious, it was a one room apartment to accommodate my son; and that was important to me. He was returning to the United States, and I had a place that was homely and affordable. I was extremely happy. My brother Steven was traveling to the United States with his basketball team and Anthony would travel back to the United States with him.

The day Anthony arrived I was elated. I was so excited to hold him again I couldn't contain my excitement. He was now walking and had teeth. I couldn't believe how much he had grown. I miss all his first milestones as a baby. His first steps must have been amazing. I thank God my mother was the recipient of those beautiful moments. This was another one of the many agonizing sacrifices I had to live with. Holding Anthony close reminded me of how much I missed being a mother. Sherman also managed a visit with Anthony, the reunion was emotional and heartwarming. I knew our time together was going to be brief, but I just wanted to immerse myself in the moment. I thank God we were together if it was just for a moment as a family. I honestly felt like a mother once more.

The next day my first motherly act was a visit to the clinic for his medical checkup. There was a lot to be grateful for. Imagine the joy when the doctor said he was growing well and was in perfect health despite being born premature. I may have missed all his milestones as an infant, however my mother had to be commended for doing such a magnificent job. I am more grateful for her than words can say.

Anthony got his immunization shots, and I left the clinic filled with gratitude and thanks. My son was physically healthy. I thank God for this blessing. After the doctor's visit we went shopping for new clothes. He had grown quite a bit since I last saw him. I purchased a few items for him, and his sister and we are now on our way back home on the B44 Bus in Brooklyn. I'm feeling good, my son is in my arms and my spirits are up. My children are being cared for by my mother and they are healthy, happy and doing wonderfully. God is really watching over my beautiful children. It was gratifying. For the first time in a long while I was in a happy place. I felt like a doting mother holding Anthony so close. I miss my children so much. I was daydreaming of being with them again. I was in the most beautiful headspace. I didn't even notice when the bus stopped, and a gentleman sat next to us. My daydreaming came to an end when he began to make small talk. Minutes later we were in deep conversation. I took his phone number and promised to stay in touch as I exited the bus. At that very moment the idea of a green card came to me. It was a long shot and also crazy, but I was willing to do anything to be with my children again.

Once I made it home, I had to strategically set up my next move. I didn't tell anyone what was in my head, because just thinking about it was mind boggling. With a heavy heart I decided to arrange for Anthony's plane ride back to Trinidad. I was grateful for the little time that God had given me with Anthony but if this plan was going to work, he had to be in Trinidad with my mother. I couldn't possibly do something this drastic with him around.

Somehow, I had to find a delicate way to ask for my passport back from the Stern's. With Anthony traveling back to Trinidad it seemed logical that I would need the passport for parental identification. Our mother and son's time together was heartwarming and beautiful, words can't describe it. When I looked into his little eyes, I could tell he needed me as much as I needed him. In that short time, once again I felt like a mother, and I knew I was going to do what it takes to be with them again. Even if it meant taking on something so risky.

At the end of the week Anthony was on his way to Trinidad. When he arrived, my mother called and said he landed safely and reunited with his sister. I was back in the Stern's kitchen the following Tuesday. It's amazing how far your mind could drift when you're engulfed with heaps of dirty laundry to wash and put away. Doing laundry could take me well into the night. While the Sterns slept, I was weaving my plan. I desperately needed this peace and quiet to strategize my next step. There was no room for failure. I was willing to take an enormous risk with a total stranger, just to be reunited with my children.

I didn't know if the stranger on the bus was willing to go along with my proposal, but I plan to ask him. I had to admit this was forward and I would come off as desperate, if the truth be told I was. I was desperately longing to be with my children again. It hurt being away from them. The emotion I felt holding my son again after so long, only ignited me to forge full steam ahead. The next week I asked Mr. Elliot if he would help me, and he said yes. I agree the Stern's house was safe and there was no doubt they would proceed with the filling process, but I needed to be with my children. I was prepared to risk it all to be reunited with them.

Marrying someone I didn't know was risky and outright dangerous, however this was the quickest way to make it back to Trinidad for my kids. After a couple of phone calls between myself and Mr. Elliot, we decided on a date and my plan was in motion. I was not going to mention it to anyone, especially my boss. The mere fact that I haven't figured out everything for myself I decided to keep my mouth shut. I thought I had it all planned out; I was going to marry this stranger and return to work. I was not thinking rationally. I was just focused on my green card and my children. I was simply a young mother yearning to be with her children. Every day I interacted with this family I saw how happy they were. I am hoping to be like them one day. Don't housekeepers deserve this kind of happiness? Well, I was going for it. Honestly, I don't know how housekeepers do it. I am not knocking anyone's hustle as a housekeeper, but I am on the hunt for more. I am going to take a chance.

A logical thinking person will not have done something like this, however when you don't have your legal documents, you tend not to think logically. My kids were depending on me to get them, and I was not about to disappoint them. I didn't have it all planned out; I was putting everything together as I went along. I was about to marry a total stranger

I didn't know, return to Long Island, and hide out in the Stern's kitchen. I would be patient until some type of working documents came through and just stayed under the radar. Just playing the scenario out in my mind seemed crazy. God help me. I knew the Stern's would advise me not to do something so drastic and outright dangerous, so I didn't tell anyone, not even my brother. I kept my crazy dream and no good plan to myself.

I took the leap of faith and forged ahead. What can I say, desperate times call for desperate measures. No guts no glory. We were married at the courthouse in Brooklyn. As soon as the ceremony was over, I raced to the Long Island Railroad train and headed back to the Sterns kitchen. I kept my day's adventure to myself. I told Mrs. Sterns I had an appointment. I dare not tell her what I had just done. No one but God knew about my marriage.

I was hoping to get to know my new husband first and then reveal the secret. While we were getting to know each other, I was building our marriage portfolio. I filed the immigration paperwork immediately, and my plan was in motion. On my day off we would be inseparable. We were slowly becoming a married couple unknowing to anyone. I am fantasizing about a real relationship, and I began to relax. The very first interview with immigration came quickly. The interview was scheduled for a Monday, my day off. I didn't have to miss a day. My secret could be kept safe. Everything went off without a hitch. The next day I made it back to the Stern's without batting an eye.

Things were going fine on the job front and I wanted to keep it that way. Back in Brooklyn the marriage was also heating up. We consummated the marriage and became husband and wife in every sense of the word. Every weekend when I came home to Brooklyn, I made sure we had pictures taken. I am thinking we are on the same page. I am working hard to get my paperwork and fees in order. Meanwhile my husband can't produce even one piece of document. Every weekend he had an excuse. When immigration sent the second appointment letter, I became increasingly nervous because there was no urgency on his part. I took the initiative in gathering medical and insurance papers. I was intent on being ready and well prepared.

We were two months away from the appointment. I started to become even more suspicious when some of his excuses just didn't make sense. When I confronted my husband, he would become illusive and angry. I began to do my own investigation and found out that my husband was not who I thought he was. The only truth I assumed that he told was that he was born in America. I don't know if he really intended to help me with my green card. I was duped. I couldn't believe it.

The signs were there but I chose to ignore them. I planned to stay on the job for the weekend. I told him I had to work extra days to make up the money for the fees. I had to wrap my mind around what was happening. My plan blew up in my face and I didn't know what to do. Who could I tell? I was so embarrassed. Thank God for the job. The Stern's home was again my place of solace and refuge. I was thankful for a place to just pull my thoughts together. I had to fully comprehend what I had done. The truth was I wanted what I had done to all go away. God knows it won't be that easy. I knew I made a horrible mistake but again, who do I tell this secret to? I am his wife. That couldn't change overnight. We already went to the first interview. How do I get out of that? It was a huge mess.

I didn't want to be anywhere near him. I had only myself to blame. In the back of my mind a voice was saying tell my boss or even my brother Steven, but I was too ashamed. One week left before our appointment. I am in Brooklyn hoping he has his documents but too afraid to ask. I didn't want to trigger him. When I arrived in Brooklyn that weekend out of nowhere, he suggested that we should take a trip down south. He saw the confused look on my face. Then he said his documents were in the south where he claimed to be from. I calmly told him I had to get my money together and had already taken too much time away from the job. He was not having any of my explanations.

I asked him what documents he had with him, and he said none. He said he would have it all when we returned from the south. I told him I just couldn't go with him. We began arguing, before I knew what was happening, we were in an outright brawl. The fight was so violent that it spilled into the hallway of the apartment building. I am truly thankful and forever grateful for the woman across the hall who called the police, because I am not sure how it would have ended. Yes, I was a fighter unfortunately for him. When the dust settled, I had a horrible blackeye and quite a few bruises. It was a hefty price to pay for being stupid. He also had bites and bruises, unfortunately not as much as me. Happily, for me he was being dragged off by the police in handcuffs.

I am glad I put up a fight and held my own. Mammy Merle would be proud. I believe if you are in a fight and you got the worst of it like I did, let the opponent know that you were there. In other words, leave a mark. This was my very first and I hope last encounter with the NYPD. Thank God there was a woman officer at the scene. She suspected I was in over my head. She informed me after the incident on how to proceed. The officer told me to show up at the precinct the next day for the report. I could not believe this happened to me. I should've known better. It was absolutely bad judgment on my part. This could have really ended in my death. That's what I got for trying to help God. I didn't want to wait, and I made an absolute mess of everything. What would my brother say? Furthermore, Sherman would not believe I did something so stupid. I was so angry at myself. Honestly, what did I expect to happen? Father God, please forgive me.

(Psalm 51:3) For I acknowledge my transgressions: and my sin is ever before me.

I could've really been killed, could you imagine if I had gone away with him? I might've ended up in a cornfield or a ditch somewhere. When I saw my face, I truly lost my mind. It was worse than I thought. I think that's what enraged me even more, as I made my way to the police precinct. I was now what you called a battered wife. I left the precinct knowing that he cannot return to my home and with a docket number from the report. On the way home I remember when the police were dragging Mr. Elliot down the halls of the apartment that he threatened never to show up to the second interview. The craziest thing was, I didn't care. For some reason I just wanted to get away from that man and wipe away every memory of ever meeting him. The fear of immigration was not as horrifying as what he had done to me. I took a high-stake risk and lost. I didn't think it through or the possible repercussions, and it almost cost me my life. My family and my children would never know the risk and the sacrifices that I made as an immigrant trying to make it in America. My desperation clouded my judgment, and I made a horrible life altering mistake. I had no one to blame but myself, I had to take full responsibility for my actions. I realize that I did this, I placed myself in this vulnerable and dangerous situation and I suffered dearly for it. I am thankful that my children were not here to see me in this state.

I couldn't go to work in that condition. My face was too messed up. No amount of makeup could conceal a black eye. I told my boss I was sick. I took a week home again and got myself together. I had to heal, and I didn't want anyone to see me like that. I was too ashamed. I was also angry that I gave him all that power over me, that he felt compelled to take advantage of me. When you are an undocumented immigrant as I was, you are viewed as prey. Some of us survive and some don't. Thanks to The Most High God I am one of the survivors. It's only by God's grace I am alive today. While I was home feeling defeated and licking my wounds, I decided to first apologize to God.

(Psalm 32:5) I acknowledged my sin unto thee, and mine iniquity have I not hid. I said, I will confess my transgressions unto the LORD; and thou forgavest the iniquity of my sin.

(Psalm 34:17-20) The righteous cry, and the LORD hearth, and delivereth out of all their troubles; The LORD is nigh unto them that are of a broken heart; and saveth such as be of a contrite spirit; Many are the affiliations of the righteous: but the LORD delivereth him out of them all; He keepeth all his bones: not one of them is broken.

I didn't let *Him* lead and it almost cost me my life. I know God was watching over me because I didn't die. My mother always says once you have life you have hope. My hope was in the Lord. *He* was a forgiving God and *He* loved me even when I made mistakes. *He* promises to bestow on me *His* grace and mercies. I prayed and asked God for *His* forgiveness and guidance. I felt compelled to gather all the documents I had on file from the marriage and send it into immigration with the police report. After running to the post office under heavy disguise, I went into hiding for the rest of the week. That week of my healing was also the week that immigration had scheduled for our second appointment. I was experiencing all these emotions; my head was reeling. How was I going to get my children now? God help me.

> *(Psalm 62:11-12) God hath spoken once; twice have I heard this; power belongeth unto God; Also unto thee, O Lord, belongeth mercy: for thou renderest to every man according to his work.*

I felt sorry for myself, but more so anger. I was angry that I didn't leave him with a deeper scar before the police got there. However, I am thankful that this didn't end with my death. That week home proved to be what I needed. I did a lot of soul-searching and I had to regroup. One thing was sure, I was never letting Mr. Elliot back into my life and home again. Furthermore, I was never going to be placed in such a vulnerable position ever again. I am praying to God daily for *His* wisdom and *His* understanding so I can be more equipped to deal with life situations and challenges. I realize that I am not smart, and I ask, no actually I begged God for discernment to make better decisions.

The emotion that followed after that frightening encounter was a daily reminder of how close I came to being harmed. What was so hurtful, was I am not quite two years in the United States and my name is already attached to the NYPD report. I could not believe the mess I have gotten myself into. The little bit of sense that I had led me back to my bible and my faith in God. It strengthened my resolve, and my confidence was boosted once again. I meditated on God's word daily and I began the slow process towards my recovery. God will indeed take your pain away there is no mistake he can't fix and no wound he can't heal even a blackeye. God's mercy heals, redeems, and restores the broken hearted. Yes, even the pain that is buried ever so deep. I thank God for *His* word and *His* divine protection because it was instrumental in my healing.

> *(Isaiah 44:22) I have blotted out, as a thick cloud, thy transgressions, and as a cloud, thy sins: return unto me; for I have redeemed thee.*

> *(Isaiah 61:7); For your shame ye shall have double; and for confusion they shall rejoice in their portion: therefore in their land they shall possess the double: everlasting joy shall be unto them.*

My God removed my guilt and shame and washed away every sin. After I pulled myself together, I realized the good news, God was with me even in the times of my trouble. *He* didn't just save me, *He* sustained me with the strength to face my daily adversities. Even though I endured beatings, whether it was spiritual, relational, emotional, physical, or mental, God never left me.

> *(Psalms 55:17-18) Evening, and morning, and at noon, will I pray, and cry aloud; and he shall hear my voice; He hath delivered my soul in peace from the battle that was against me: for there were many with me.*

I remembered that I was made in the image of God's likeness. I understand that whatsoever I endured in life, I had faith that God was going to strengthen me. *His* grace was sufficient. Now I am ready, willing, and able to face any challenge.

Returning to work was rough but now I was most appreciative of a place to really hide out and pull my thoughts together. I absolutely wasn't going to tell the Stern's what happened. I was too ashamed, and they wouldn't believe me anyway. There were days I was tired, and the house was so huge, but I pushed on. *His* grace kept me. The words of Mr. Elliot would not leave my head. His threat of not showing up for the next interview had me thinking. Did he really have the power to destroy my dreams of bringing my daughter to America? How was I going to turn this around? The answer was to just trust God, *He* is the miracle worker not me.

The Bible said plainly what the devil meant for evil God would turn out for my good. It was about two months after the horrible fight. I arrived home from work and opened the mailbox. There was a large manila envelope addressed to me from immigration. Now my nerves are on overdrive. I'm shaking and sweating all at the same time. I slowly opened it; Lord help me! To my disbelief, every piece of documents that I sent to immigration office came back. Attached to the very last page was the coveted green card. I went into shock, God brought me through, thank you Jesus.

> *(Psalm 52:8-9) But I am like a green olive tree in the house of God: I trust in the mercy of God for ever and ever; I will praise thee for ever, because thou hast done it: and I will wait on thy name; for it is good before thy saints.*

I had a black and blue eye for almost a week, but God gave me a green card for my lifetime. This indeed was the process to the promotion. Even in my darkest days in America I trusted and hoped in the Lord. I am not proud of the decision I made, I was frustrated, desperate and anxious and I acted on these negative emotions. The end result was disastrous. I am thankful to The Most High God for keeping me under the shadow of *His* wings. *He* did promise to take away my shame. For your shame Debbie you shall have double. I was downtrodden and experienced one of the most difficult and challenging times in my life and The Most High God brought me out as pure gold. *He* heard my cry, and My God delivered me. This was the second miracle I experienced while in America. God is truly a miracle worker, and my trust is only in *Him*.

> *(Proverbs 3:5-6) Trust in the LORD with all thine heart: and lean not unto thine own understanding; In all thy ways acknowledge him, and he shall direct thy path.*

PHOTO GALLERY

First apartment while preparing for my son Anthony's
return to the United States.

Sherman and our son
Anthony reunited.

Below:
My brother Steven
bringing Anthony back
from Trinidad.

CHAPTER 5

The Dreamer Going Home

It's 1990, Three years later after all the fantasizing and dreaming in the Stern's laundry room, I am on my way back to Trinidad with a green card. Back then this was unheard of. You could not get a green card that quickly unless your parents filed the paperwork. This was what you call a modern-day miracle, and I can only say God is real and *He* is a rewarder of them who diligently seek him. Landing in Trinidad and seeing my mother and daughter, was indeed a gift from God. I was still in shock. Most people thought I was deported back. No one could believe I had my green card.

Everyone was asking how, and all I could tell them was *WHO*; The Almighty God.

> *(Romans 8:31) What can we then say to these things? If God be for us, who can be against us?*

My time was short in Trinidad, but you know what, I didn't care. My main focus was still the same, to be with my kids. Seeing my children together was amazing. I got to hold them close and kiss them. I just felt whole again. My mother told me she was proud of me and that was all I needed to hear. Leaving Latonya again would be heartbreaking, because I was taking Anthony back to the United States. The heartbreak wasn't going to be for too long, because I knew I could return to Trinidad any time to visit her. However, there was an urgency to finish what I set out to accomplish, and that was to have her with me. I had to resubmit her immigration documents, that was a major setback for me, but God would make a way. I promise to allow *Him* to lead me, and I pray that I have learned my lesson.

Back in New York the baby's father's situation was not going how he wanted. He also got married for his green card, however his situation was far different and more difficult than mine. He couldn't work and hide out in someone's kitchen as I did. He had to remain in the shadows until he got his paperwork. Sometimes he will take a chance and work with his cousin Tony on various construction sites and hope to keep his illegal status under wraps. I earnestly prayed for his breakthrough. I honestly didn't want to ruin his chances of him never seeing his mother again. I swallowed the bitter pill and stayed clear but continued to pray for his breakthrough.

I worked for the Stern's until they found a new babysitter. After years of working for that family, I can truly say my hunch about them was right. They were wonderful and I was blessed to have known them. I will never forget that family. I thank God for placing me with them in that unsteady season of my life. We parted on good terms and promised to stay in touch. I was spreading my wings and I don't think I could do it with a mop and broom. I wanted to further my education and Anthony had to be in daycare. I had to find employment outside. Needless to say, they will always have a special place in my heart. I moved from cleaning the house to selling chicken. I found a new hustle at KFC. The money was small, but I had to do something to pay the bills. I needed a job that would provide the flexibility that I needed. I enrolled Anthony in daycare, and I returned to what I knew best, books. This job was ideal because it accommodated my classes. Yes, I enrolled in classes for my G.E.D. I worked hard at it, studying late at night and working hard at KFC. I had dreams of attending college. Yes, I was a dreamer. I believe you can never stop dreaming.

I desperately needed to improve my resume to continue the immigration paperwork for my daughter. Babysitting was the only job I had. It was crucial that I improve my financial status and my education credentials. KFC's salary was small, but it would have to do until I got something better. I was elated when I got the results of my G.E.D, I passed with high scores. "Hallelujah". Better finally came, it came by way of the United States Post Office located on 34th Street. I am really moving up now.

I can now raise the money to file for Latonya. The post office job was hard, but I liked it, because it gave me status. I needed to impress immigration. Debbie is a postal worker.

This is not a dream. I was hired as a casual or seasonal worker. I didn't mind what title it was, immigration just wanted to know that I had a steady income, and I could financially support my daughter. I could not believe this, immigrant Debbie just landed in America, and she's now a postal worker. This is really the land of opportunity. I am certainly not going to let my opportunity go to waste.

I felt prestigious, not to mention this job would definitely boost my resume. I felt a sense of gratitude. God bless me with the talent of reading, and I am going to work hard to enhance my talent and put it to use. I am using my reading skills for the United States mail. Imagine that. Father it really does pay to dream. I enjoyed the job, and the checks made a world of difference. Money for Latonya's paperwork is beginning to grow. I was only six months into the job when I got the news that it was ending. I was devastated. I was going up the ladder and fell off. This was a stable income, enough to get my daughter's paperwork completed and in a blink of an eye it was gone. I cried for days, I just felt it was worth crying over so I did. After moping around for a few more days I had to move on, and bills had to be paid. One door closes and I know God will open another. I had to believe that God is working it out for my good. I began to encourage myself, Debbie, no more crying, no more fear.

(Romans 8:28) And we know that all things work together for good to them that love God, to them who are the called according to his purpose.

The new year is here, it's 1991, and the holidays are over. I decided to wipe my tears and step out on faith. I enrolled in college. You know you're rolling on faith when you start college without a dollar. I knew God was covering me. He was leading, so I am following. I decided to attend New York City Technical College. It sounded prestigious, so why not. Sitting in the classroom after all those years really intimidated me. God didn't give me the spirit of fear, so I pushed on. I was placed in remedial classes. Imagine the shame, don't these people know that I went to private school. Remedial classes or not, all I could think of was Debbie in college. I am going places; you just watch me.

As the weeks passed my confidence grew. I realize the West Indies school system was quite different. I now had to study American history, African American history, sociology, and politics, and various other classes. These foreign systems only made me thirsty for more. The shame of remedial classes was not going to be for much longer. In so many ways this ground level start was a blessing for me moving forward.

Once I completed the remedial classes, I could register for accredited courses. So, I pushed on. I decided to find my way back to KFC. I had no other choice. I needed cash, no matter how small. God knew my heart, all I needed was his strength. At the college there were a lot of postings for state and city jobs. I picked out a few I could afford, and I decided I will pay for the tests. I filled out as many applications as I could and just waited. I knew my big break would come, but first I had to further my education. I had to make myself marketable and then take it to the next level. I had a full plate. Back in the 90s all the possibilities and opportunities were there, you just had to have the drive and the desire. No more limitation or intimidation, I was forging ahead on God's strength. I placed all my confidence and full dependency on *Him*. All I saw was empowerment. I was emboldened to move forward without fear.

(Philippians 1:6) Being confident of this very thing, that he which hath begun a good work in you will perform it until the day of Jesus Christ.

Things are moving fast now for Sherman. He finally got his green card with the marriage his cousin had arranged for him. He said in a couple of months he would be returning home to Trinidad to visit his mother. This was wonderful for Sherman. He was well on his way to helping his mother and providing a better life for his son. I know when he returned to Trinidad his mother would be happy to see him. The reunion would be amazing. I remember how it was for me. God was really working things out in his favor. With his green card he could travel and move around without fear of immigration. The year definitely started off great for Sherman. When he returned from Trinidad, he immediately started his job search. He planned on helping his mom migrate to the US. He also wanted to help out more with Anthony. Sherman knew I was really struggling. Everyone had to pull their weight if we were going to provide for our son in a meaningful way. We agreed he would take Anthony to the daycare so I could get to my early classes. Only God knew how I survived the fast-moving pace of raising a child, attending school, and working in America. Some days it was rough, but God had a plan and a purpose for me to prosper and I thank *Him*.

> *(Psalm 128:2) For thou shalt eat the labour of thine hands: happy shalt thou be, and it shall be well with thee.*

PHOTO GALLERY

Debbie taking a bath at the roadside in Trinidad.

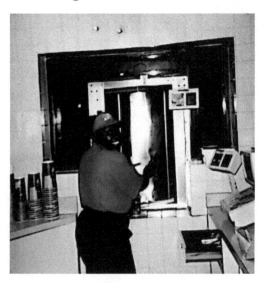

Happy to have a job at KFC making $2.75 an hour.

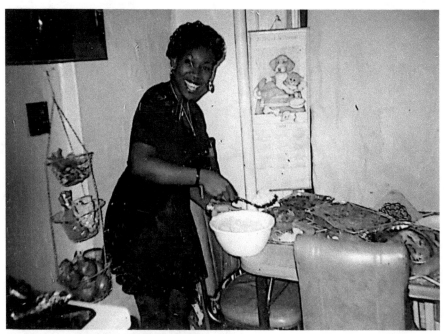

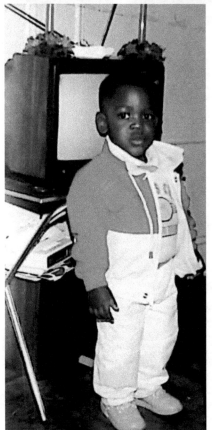

Humble beginnings and
Anthony's going to day
care.

CHAPTER 6

Gone to Soon

I didn't anticipate it being so hard, but God promised to sustain me once I kept my eyes on *Him*. *He* was the wind beneath my sail. This semester was grueling. I had to work later hours to accommodate my classes. Sometimes I was studying in the lunchroom at KFC. This was not the best schedule or accommodations however, it was necessary. Sherman was trying to make his way up the ladder, it was a tremendous struggle for everyone. I was anticipating a well deserved break. I was so tired. This was my last day of finals. I am so anxious I can't wait for it to be over.

Sherman had picked up Anthony and left for the daycare, so I was getting ready for class. The phone rang, and it was Chris, Sherman's other cousin's wife. She blurted out that Sherman had been shot. I was not sure I heard right, I told her I didn't hear her, and her response was Sherman was shot a few minutes ago. I was speechless. I was trying to speak, and no words were coming out. Sherman had just picked up Anthony to take him to daycare not too long ago, how could he be shot? Chris said she will call me back with more information. My head is spinning. I am rushing to get dressed to get to the daycare and maybe get some understanding of what's happening. The phone rang again before I could say a word. Chris said Sherman didn't make it, he is dead. God help us all.

Fortunately for Anthony, Sherman had just dropped him off at the daycare. He lived two blocks away. Sherman returned home and was at his door with his car keys in his hand when someone shot him multiple times. I was inconsolable. I cried on the bus all the way to the daycare. I was an emotional wreck when I got to Anthony. What happened to his father was unimaginable. Everything we had

86

dreamed of went away in minutes. How could this happen? Who would want to kill Sherman? So many questions and no one to answer them. I just wanted to hold my son. God knows this was too much for a four-year-old child. We arrived at Sherman's aunt's house, and everyone was gathered there. Bewilderment and sadness were on everyone's face. Reality had set in. My four-year-old son's father, Sherman Superville is dead. He just got his green card, went home, visited his mother and now he was shot down in the streets of New York so violently. He didn't deserve this. Father God help us.

I could not study for finals. I didn't want a failing grade, so I did what I could do to get through it. By the next week I was packing to travel to Trinidad for Sherman's funeral. I was moving in a robotic state. I just couldn't function. I didn't know what to do. What do you tell a four-year-old at a time like this? How could he die like that? What is happening Lord, what is happening! I cried out to the Lord again.

We landed in Trinidad and went directly to his mother's house. It was heartbreaking to see her in so much pain. How in heaven's name could Sherman be dead, she had just seen him a few months ago. All his dreams and aspirations were wiped away. There were no words, just tears. The funeral was one of the saddest times in my life. I think Anthony might be scarred for life. With the loss of a parent so violently you really don't know the psychological effect it will have on a four-year-old child. The guilt and pain from this tragedy was tearing me apart. I had a personal stake in this. Sherman Superville came to be with us. After everything he went through to arrive in America, then the hurdles for his green card now he is dead. Father God none of this makes any sense. Seeing Latonya again was the only upside to this devastating tragedy. At least I was able to hold her once again.

The return trip back to the US was a horrible one. I was drained. I couldn't attend classes, so I decided no school for me. I walked around in a tunnel of grief. The pain was overwhelming. Some days it felt that I could not see God. I kept calling on God to remove the pain and *He* just wouldn't answer. How could *He* take him away from us? I had to get my head together. I was unraveling. Thanks to my brother who literally helped us cope with the tragedy. Steven was the one that stepped in as we digested this devastating loss. He was instrumental in helping us through those rough days. With his assistance, Anthony's routine was not disrupted, although our lives were turned upside down. I had to maintain some sort of normalcy for Anthony. I prayed that interaction with the other children at the daycare would serve as a distraction for him. Steven promised to fill the gap the best way he could, and we tried to make Anthony's life as normal as possible.

(Psalm 130:1-2,5) Out of the depths have I cried unto thee, O LORD. Lord, hear my voice: let thine ears be attentive to the voice of my supplication. I wait for the LORD, my soul doth wait, and in his word do I hope.

We didn't have everything worked out; however, we did what we could just to get through the days. My son was fatherless, that was our new reality. I prayed for the year to end and start fresh. I wanted to get back to school. Apart from my children, school made me feel alive and in my right mind. I needed to be rescued, and books were my life raft.

Registering for classes really brought me back to my true self. I could have benefited with some hours of therapy, but I could not afford it. So, I just waited for God to shine *His* face on me once more. I was now working more hours at KFC. With Sherman gone I had to bring in more cash. I missed the deadline for college work study, so I ultimately had to return and work for the Stern's. I travel to Long Island to cook and clean every Friday before the Sabbath. I would arrive early with recipes already laid out and start cooking while doing the laundry. The bedrooms were cleaned, vacuumed and all linen changed. The house was spick and span, and I was back on the Long Island Railroad to pick up my shift for 6 pm at KFC. How we made it through the fall of 1992, I don't know. I realize God never removed the pain. *He* just gave me the grace to sustain it. The money was not growing fast enough, but we made what we had work. I was looking forward to the new year because Anthony will be starting preschool. I knew there will be many difficult days ahead however God was my keeper. My New Year's prayer was for God to change the atmosphere and give us a better year than the last. Rest in Peace Sherman. We will meet again.

In 1993, it started off with everyone in some type of school, I was now laser focused on my education. I had to get a better job and education was the key. I even dared to dream of a better apartment. I was also pushing for my daughter to get out of Trinidad sooner than later. With Sherman gone I had to work twice as hard to stay afloat. With God all things are possible you just have to believe. I believe God would guide me through this once I kept my eyes focused on *Him*. I channeled my energy on the few positive things in my life; my children and school, and I asked God to change my pain to peace. I was determined, and in the face of all my adversities I persevered. It was only by God's grace.

(Psalm 135:5-6) For I know that the LORD is great, and that our Lord is above all gods. Whatsoever the LORD pleased, that did he in heaven, and in earth, in the seas, and all deep places.

The tide began to turn for us, I am a few classes away from my very first degree. Anthony is headed to grade school and 1 found a basement apartment. To top it off I met someone who happened to catch my eye on the job. We had a lot in common, he struggled to get a better job than KFC and move out of the projects. I myself have the same dreams of a better job and a nice home. He also attended New York City Technical College and is striving to continue his college experience. I felt I was really in good company.

The relationship moved quickly because we were together on the job at KFC almost every day. It was not long before we were sharing our new basement apartment. Yes, we got an apartment together. I think he really wanted to flee the projects. I just wanted to have someone in my life with the same views and future goals, and most importantly a father figure for my kids. Mr. Shaw was perfect. Working hard was all he knew and there was no shame in any job. We had so much in common, it's like I was looking in a mirror. All I was praying for now was for immigration to call. Getting my daughter with me is the only missing piece of the puzzle. I am asking God to keep me patient and focus.

> *(Proverbs 8:34) Blessed is the man that heareth me, watching daily at my gates, waiting at the posts of my doors.*

PHOTO GALLERY

Gone to Soon:
Sherman's Funeral.

In Loving Memory of

SHERMAN F. SUPERVILLE

May 12, 1992

Our father who art in heaven, Hallowed be thy name, Thy Kingdom come. Thy will be done on earth as it is in heaven. Give us this day our daily bread. And forgive us our debts, as we forgive our debtors. And lead us not into temptation, but deliver us from evil. For Thine is the Kingdom, and the power, and the glory, forever. Amen.

House of Hills, Inc.
Funeral Homes

1000 St. John's Place, Brooklyn, NY
406 Rogers Avenue, Brooklyn, NY
(718) 773-0014

93

CHAPTER 7

Completion

It was early in the year when I was handed the large envelope by the landlord, with the words immigration and naturalization. Those large envelopes always made me nervous. My heart is beating so fast I could hardly contain my excitement. My sweaty palms couldn't even open the envelope. My daughter's paperwork was finally approved. Thankfully my dream of returning home to Trinidad for my daughter has become a reality. Imagine the excitement. God is good. It took seven years of struggling with immigration, but God promised, and God never goes back on his word.

(Isaiah 55:11-12) So shall my word be that goeth forth out of my mouth: it shall not return unto me void, but it

shall accomplish that which I please, and it shall prosper in the thing whereto I sent it; For ye shall go out with joy, and be led forth with peace: the mountains and the hills shall break forth before you into singing, and all the trees of the field shall clap their hands.

Some days it seemed like I was going backwards. I was thrown so many curveballs that I often became frustrated, but I never gave up. I had to admit that the fight for my daughter sometimes felt impossible. However, what seemed impossible with man was proven possible with God. The ordeal brought me to the realization that I had to trust God and wait. I have learned from my past mistakes to never go ahead of God. I trust *Him* and *His* promises towards me. I thank God I never gave up. I stayed the course, and we were victorious in the end. There was indeed a blessing in my obedience.

(Ephesians 3:20) Now unto him that is able to do exceedingly abundantly above all that we ask or think, according to the power that worketh in us.

As parents we all make sacrifices and leaving Latonya behind was one of them. I was not the only mother that left their kids behind. I had friends who were in the same agonizing situation. My school mate Denise was also struggling to get her daughter to the United States. Denise made me promise that whenever I was given the opportunity to bring Latonya out of Trinidad, I would not leave her daughter behind. I managed to arrange the flight to get to Trinidad, thank God everything went smoothly. On June 29, 1994, I finally got my daughter to the United States. I kept my promise and Denise was reunited with her daughter Gene. God showed me favor and compassion all through these years, so I had to return the blessing to someone else. I know the emotions of leaving a child behind.

I know firsthand what it feels like leaving and looking into the child's teary eyes and the feeling of abandonment on their face. I felt compelled to help Denise. Her family had already taken care of her daughter's visa, so I just had to get her on the plane. Imagine praying all these years for a breakthrough for my daughter and here I am on the plane with both our daughters. I was honored and thankful that God showered us with such a wonderful blessing. I Give God Glory. He promised to fight all my battles. Anthony finally reunited with his sister, and I kept my word to my mother. I promised to return for Latonya, and I did. It took seven years, longer than I anticipated, however we are together in the end. It could only be God. The goodness of God was on full display. In the Bible, the number 7 represents completion so my struggle for Latonya's documents is now complete. All thanks and praise to God.

> *(Jerimiah 31:16-17) Thus saith the LORD; Refrain thy voice from weeping, and thine eyes from tears: for thy work shall be rewarded, saith the Lord; and they shall come again from the land of the enemy; And there is hope in thine end, saith the LORD, that thy children shall come again to their border.*

There are a lot of parents who were never able to return for their children because of unforeseen circumstances and my heart goes out with empathy for them. Everyone's journey and challenges are not the same. I could only say it had to be the Lord who showed me divine favor. I was one of the fortunate ones that survived the struggles and various adversities. To all those mothers and fathers that make the sacrifice of leaving a child or children behind, continue in the struggle but allow God to lead the way. Don't give up, keep fighting and like me

God will make a way and you will return one day. I returned, I can proudly say I am one of those mothers that left their child behind, but to God be the glory I returned. We were finally together, and we made up for all the lost years. We had the summer for the record books. We were eager to make up for the years that we were separated.

I felt like my life was finally coming together. I really didn't want the summer to end. It was a wonderful summer with both my children. While we were having a fun summer Latonya was familiarizing herself with the neighborhood. It was important for her to learn quickly because she would be starting school in September. I would always be grateful for that summer. It was the summer of new beginnings.

When September rolled around Latonya was registered and ready for school. Another memorable moment. It was amazing, I have both of my children in school. Thank You God. Things were moving great with Mrs. Shaw. We were looking forward to the new year. God was really looking down on me. I landed a job at Brooklyn Developmental Center. This was a group home for mentally challenged young people. It was different and it required patience and compassion to work there. The blessing that has been bestowed on me by The Almighty God, I felt that I had to be excellent in this position. This job made me appreciate life and health. I was thankful for the job, I felt that everything was finally falling into place. This new job meant an increase in my salary, and I don't have to rush to Long Island anymore. I can slow my pace down and focus on graduating and making my way out of the basement. Mr. Shaw and I decided we were committed to saving every penny so we can focus on buying our dream house. We have come a long way from KFC.

When Mr. Shaw got hired at BDC it was no surprise, I made sure he knew everything about the facility. When it was time for the interview, he was flawless with his answers. It was like the good old days. It's funny how we always end up working together. He worked the evening shift, and I worked in the morning. We had a goal and worked hard towards it. We worked nonstop. We were focused and driven. Saving for our home was our number one priority. We dubbed 1995 as the year of saving. We knew by the new year we would be ready to enter the house hunting market. We were confident that we could bid on an affordable home. Our days of hard work and intense saving were bringing us closer to our dream house. The Good Lord was really smiling on me because here comes another blessing.

> *(Psalms 13:6) I will sing unto the LORD, because he hath dealt bountifully with me.*

> *(Proverbs 10:22) The blessing of the LORD, it maketh rich, and he addeth no sorrow with it.*

PHOTO GALLERY

The girls coming to America on the plane for the first time.

CHAPTER 8

MTA Letter

I was on the job at BDC for only one year when I got the letter. The letter was from the New York City Transit Authority. Yes, I said MTA, I had totally forgotten that I had taken the test. The letter stated that I was assigned a training class on March 31, 1996. This was my mother's birthday. I am convinced she was praying for me. I was so happy. I am now an MTA employee. I knew the MTA was a big deal, but I just didn't imagine the magnitude of this company. There were a lot of rules and regulations to follow, however once you maintained probation for one year you were set for life; I mean set. The job offered a pension, health and dental benefits and the biggest perk of all was your MetroCard. As an employee for MTA, I had the privilege of riding the trains, buses and even Long Island Railroad free of charge. Not to be out done, employees were represented by one of the strongest Unions, Local 100.

If you ask me, I hit the jackpot. Lord I am grateful, thank you. To be hired at this time of my life was the ultimate breakthrough. I remembered not too long ago I was on the Long Island Railroad heading to the Sterns to clean their house; and now I am in a MTA uniform riding for free. That could only be God.

This high paying job would definitely position us in the direction of our new home. I literally didn't know the magnitude of MTA until years later. There were so many avenues to follow it was astonishing. I had no time to figure out what I was going to do with BDC. I was working two jobs, city and state paying good money. I couldn't wrap my head around it.

I am about to lose my mind. I came from selling chicken at KFC with a salary of $2.75 an hour. Now I am employed for the state and city at the same time in America. Somebody hit me over the head because I'm dreaming. No, if it's a dream don't wake me.

Eventually I would have to walk away from one, but not yet. I will work until it becomes too difficult. I ask God to give me the strength. I was able to secure a nice down payment for our dream house. I must admit the run was a good one, but ultimately, I walked away from Brooklyn Developmental Center (BBC) and stayed with New York City Transit. This turned out to be one of the best decisions I have ever made in my adult life. All I can say is, working for New York City Transit was the catalyst for getting myself and my children out of the basement. Give God Glory.

Talk about starting from the ground up. Well Debbie started from the basement. That hole in the ground was not going to be the story of my life. I heard someone say a long time ago it's not where you start it is where you finish.

(Psalm 37: 4-5) Delight thyself also in the LORD: and he shall give thee the desires of thine heart; Commit thy ways unto the LORD; trust also in him; and he shall bring it to pass.

God said *He* will order my footsteps. With a down payment saved Mr. Shaw and I began looking at the housing market. I was literally on cloud nine, things could not be better. I am counting down to the end of probation and anticipating the salary increase. This increase puts us in a better position for the housing market. Things were moving nicely, so we decided to take a well-deserved vacation. We treated ourselves to a trip to Trinidad for Carnival.

PHOTO GALLERY

Debbie working for the MTA.

CHAPTER 9

Diamond in the Rough

We were working so hard we were looking forward to this trip. It was Mr. Shaw's first trip to Trinidad and the excitement is on. Our prospects for home ownership are looking good, so there was cause for celebration. The stay in Trinidad was wonderful. We enjoyed Trinidad Carnival to the fullest. The only downside was it was too short. We knew we would not have another vacation anytime soon, so we painted the town red, white and black.

Once we returned home, we picked up where we left off with overtime. My shift changed, and the job was now sending me to Manhattan stations. Those stations were much busier and a lot harder. I was feeling fatigued and lightheaded. I just assumed I was working too hard or maybe the sudden change in schedule was to blame. I made an appointment with the doctor at the Hip Center. After the examination and litany of tests the doctor said it might be fibroids. He sent me to the hospital for further tests. The doctor at the Hip Center was right. I was diagnosed with fibroids at the hospital but that was not all, the doctors also found a heartbeat. I was pregnant.

I'm thinking this can't be happening now. I just got my dream job. I'm freaking out while Mr. Shaw is jumping for joy. Wow a baby! Now house hunting was priority number one. No way my baby was coming into this world and heading into a basement. Ten years ago, I had a baby on someone's used couch which also served as my bed, located in the hallway. I was adamant that this would not be the case for this pregnancy. I was determined to move up and move out. My due date was late December, so we had time to find a nice affordable home. Unfortunately, it was not in the stars for me. The only explanation I could muster up was, it was not my season. When I said things went bad, it is an understatement.

As the pregnancy progressed the house hunting decreased. Mr. Shaw seems to be changing. No more excitement of a new house and baby. He went from a happy expecting dad to some restless caged human I couldn't recognize. I was confused and didn't know what to do. I am thinking it's the pregnancy or my hormones that were giving me these emotions. One minute we're excited about the new baby and finding a new home and the next minute he is spending all his time at his mother's house. I didn't pick up on the signs. I was oblivious to what was going on. I needed help and I needed it quickly. My mother couldn't come immediately. So, I had to suffer in silence and battle on during the final months of my pregnancy. I prayed to God to keep me in my right mind. As I was nearing the due date the doctor said it was time to stop working and rest.

I prayed for help. I knew God would eventually send help, but I had to be patient. My sister would be here just before the delivery; even that little morsel of support would have to do. Although Mr. Shaw is acting strange and distant, I had to remain calm if I wanted to ensure a safe delivery. At all costs I had to protect my unborn child and pretend to the other children that everything was normal. God are You there? Please help me.

> *(Psalm 31:16) Make thy face to shine upon thy servant: save me for thy mercies' sake.*

I had to be realistic, my dream of getting out of the basement immediately went on hold. In my heart I prayed that this time it would be a dream deferred and not a dream denied. The reality of struggling again with another newborn was definitely starting to scare me. The fear of another horrifying delivery also rested on my mind. I was an emotional wreck, but God *was* my anchor. Even if it felt as if God was not hearing me, I am convinced *He* kept me from losing my mind. I had to praise *Him* even if I didn't see *Him*. *His* grace was sufficient. *He* wouldn't give me the heavy weight if *He* didn't think I could carry it. *He* made intercession for me.

> *(Psalm 27:13) I had fainted, unless I had believed to see the goodness of the LORD in the land of the living.*

As I was nearing the due date God sent the angel. This angel flew in from Canada. My younger sister Prudy was the support I needed in this crucial time; she not only watched my back, but she was my shoulder to cry on. I was grateful to have family in my corner. Prudy confirmed my suspicion. I was not losing my mind, or the pregnancy was making me suspicious and crazy, this man was seeing someone else. Once my suspicions were proven accurate, I had a reality check. I literally stopped crying and started praying, planning, and preparing for the arrival of my baby. I had to keep focus and allow God to steady the ship. I looked to the Lord from whence cometh my help.

As I lay in the bed ready for the doctors to perform the dreaded c-section, I engaged in a lot of soul-searching. My son was born in 1988 under stress. It is now 1997, almost ten years later and it seems I am walking the same road of uncertainty and instability. I knew this feeling. It's not normal. I needed to speak to someone, but I suppressed it. I didn't want anyone to know what I was going through. I kept it all in and delivered Diamond, a healthy baby girl one day before the year end. I opted to have an epidural delivery. I wanted to be wide awake and involved in the birth of my precious Diamond. While I was awake and in my right mind, I told the doctors to proceed with the Tubal ligation procedure on their way out. Yes, I had my tubes tied.

This was never going to happen to me again. Sometimes I question myself how I could be so foolish unlike other relationships this one was like a train ran over me; no pun intended. Imagine the year started with such fanfare: vacationing, house hunting, making plans to raise the baby and maybe get married. Now I have to walk out of Long Island College Hospital dejected. With my stomach bandage up from stitches, a baby in tow, and yes we are headed back to the basement. I was numb, not from the pain medication but from what I had to endure. Why put me through all that stress? I just could not make sense of it all. I felt abandoned and used. I just had to smile and keep it all in. Lord, where are you?

> *(1 Corinthian 10:13) There hath no temptation taken you but such as is common to man: but God is faithful, who will not suffer you to be tempted above that ye are able; but will with the temptation also make a way to escape, that ye may be able to bear it.*

I pretended I was not in pain as I physically and psychologically suffered in silence. Now I am in the basement with two children, a newborn and no baby daddy. Thank God my sister Prudy was there she ran interference for me. I was well within my rights to check myself into the G Building (Psychiatric ward) at Kings County Hospital, but I didn't. I checked into the Knee Building (daily prayer) in the basement instead. I got on my knees and took it all to the Lord in prayer. I can truly say I prayed hard and prevented myself from falling prey to postpartum depression.

> *(Psalm 30:10) Hear, O LORD, and have mercy upon me: LORD, be thou my helper.*
>
> *(Psalm 34:4) I sought the LORD, and he heard me, and delivered me from all my fears.*

My sister only stayed an extra few days so I could pull myself together. It was not much time, but I had no way of keeping her with me. She had to return to her job in Canada. I thank God I had my sister in that horrible season in my life. Once my sister left, I realized how much I needed her, I had become totally dependent on her. I am alone with three children in a basement that was supposed to be a new house. I just felt lost and sorry for myself. I was praying and it seemed that God was not hearing me. I was not just worried about me, but my children were also suffering. I was plunging into a dark depressive state once again. I could not take it anymore. I had to get my mother here quickly. I was starting to unravel, no more faking, I needed help. I needed my mother. Thank God I stayed on my knees because God kept me.

> *(Psalm 94:17) Unless the LORD hath been my help, my soul had almost dwelt in silence.*

My mother finally came to my rescue. Mammy Merle took care of Anthony 10 years ago now she was coming to help me with another baby 10 years later. My mother's presence was a Godsend. I knew the year was going to be tough, so I had to mentally prepare myself. My Mother's presence kept me sane. This time I had to believe God's word that he will never leave me nor forsake me. Once God is on the boat, I will make it through *THIS* storm. The presence of my mother motivated me. My mother made me realize I had to help myself. I had to stop feeling like a victim and believe even as bad as it is, I will be victorious. While feeling sorry for myself I didn't see my blessings staring me in the face. A beautiful, healthy baby with ten fingers and ten toes, and most importantly a mother to help with the baby and the children. I was blessed and truly grateful.

The children were really the driving force for me. The promise of a new house and their own room fell apart and I felt like I let them down. However, I was going to find a way in this wilderness to keep my promise. I had to first remove the resentment I had for the basement and turn it into thankfulness. I will admit I felt abandoned when I left Long Island College Hospital, however I had to prove to my children that we were abandoned by man but not forgotten by The Almighty God. It was in my darkest times in the basement, I realize only God can help me. I experienced rejection, rage, regret, and wanted revenge. However, as I continued to pray and call upon God, I remembered *His* promises to redeem, restore and renew. Yes, my God promised to never leave me. I had to escape from the bitter baby mama syndrome to the awesome woman that God created me to be.

(Psalm 145:14) The LORD upholdeth all that fall, and raiseth up all those that be bowed down.

I came to the realization that I had brought three children into this world, and it was my responsibility to provide and nurture them. No more feeling sorry for myself. After going through those traumatic stages I had to make a turn. I made that turn with God holding my hand. God rescued me. I humbly allowed myself to be cared for by the Lord. With *His* help I was taking my life back and reclaiming my identity.

It was the year 1998 and it could not end fast enough for me. I was in recovery mode so that meant work. No more shame, no more hiding behind the curtains. I told myself if you wanted to get out of the basement and get a house, I would have to do it myself. I remembered reading in the bible that King David had to encourage himself many times and that's what I did. I decided to encourage myself. My mother held me down while I worked. Thank God for Mammy Merle. Soon she will be leaving again, therefore I was going to make use of her support and her help with the children. I worked extra days to play catch-up for the days I missed. School had to go on the back burner so I could focus if I was going to get my children out of the basement. It was sad to say but school was the farthest thing from my mind. There was no room for failure. I knew buying a house with one income seemed impossible, however My God only deals with impossibilities.

(Luke 18:27) And he said, The things which are impossible with men are possible with God.

I knew the God I served, so I was not going to be deterred. The Prophet, Isaiah said "If I was willing and obedient, I would eat the good of the land." So, I was going to push forward.

My mother's time to leave had come. It was a sad time, and very emotional but she did the best for me, and I thanked her dearly. Now I had to stand on my own two feet. Her advice was clear, hold onto Jesus. Look to the hills from whence cometh your help and allow God to fight my battles.

(Psalm 121:1-2) I will lift up mine eyes unto the hills, from whence cometh my help; My help cometh from the LORD, which made heaven and earth.

The baby was now heading to daycare. I didn't know what I was going to do without my mother, but I took her advice and stayed close to God. I keep asking myself why I keep falling into these horrible life altering situations. Here I was feeling sorry for myself again. It was so easy to be swallowed into self-pity and depressive thoughts. Focus Debbie focus! As the days wore on, I realized this is just life. It has its ups, and it has its downs, it has its sunny days, and it has its rainy days. How I made it through is what matters. I am prepared to ride out the storm in the name of Jesus. Didn't these people know I went to private school. I had to stop telling myself and let it be known to others. I went to God again, Father, I desperately need help. I threw myself at the mercy of the LORD. I felt that at this point I had nothing to lose. I realize God was indeed carrying me all this time. Even when I thought I was not going to make it, *He* was carrying me under *His* wings.

> *(Psalm 91:11) For He shall give His angels charge over thee, to keep thee in all thy ways. (Psalm 84:11) For the LORD God is a sun and shield: the LORD will give grace and glory: no good thing will he withhold from them that walk uprightly.*

One day out of nowhere I got a response from one of the many Housing Seminars. They were having an open house and accepting applications. I mentioned the event to Marcia, Anthony's Godmother and I told her I didn't think I was ready. Marcia encouraged and then persuaded me to attend the seminar. Marcia's words were the boost I needed. I attended the seminar and filled out the application. I realize God doesn't wait for you to be ready. *His* time is not my time, and *His* ways are not my ways. I trusted God and sent in the application for a two-family home. I thank God for sending Marcia to encourage me. With 1998 coming to an end, I prayed it would end on a positive note. I filed the application and I credit Marcia Pierre to this day for what happened next. It was not even two weeks when I received a response letter. I had to send in some documents and wait for further notification. I trusted God to bless me and my children with a new home and it was coming to fruition. We would have to spend another Christmas in the basement, but God promised to reward me and renew my strength and *He* never goes back on *His* word. I just had to be patient. God promised to make a way in the wilderness. One month later in January 1999 I got the confirmation that my application was accepted. There was a lot of skepticism that a single person couldn't purchase a home, it was that difficult, however they didn't know I was never single. God was always with me.

(2 Samuel 22:33) God is my strength and power: and he maketh my way perfect; Verse 34; He maketh my feet like hinds' feet: and setteth me upon my high places.

My dream of owning a home came through. I had one month to come up with the necessary documents and a cashier's check for the down payment. I could hardly contain the excitement. I was on cloud nine. The process for closing on the house was going to be a couple months away. I was more than willing to wait. This period gave me time to gather more cash and to prepare my documents for closing on the house. God does answer prayers.

I found out in that basement that my night season had a purpose. I had to humble myself and submit to God. Somehow, I needed God to free me from the resentment I had for the basement and my daughter's father. Before I was blinded by hate and anger and allowed it to devour me. I was heartbroken and scared and I can admit I had lost my way. However, once I became thankful for my wonderful children, a healthy baby, and a place to call home, I was confident in due time God would increase my space. God will enlarge my territory. I also began the process of forgiveness. I petition God to show me how to forgive. First myself and then my daughter's father. I had to get to that place of forgiveness then thankfulness. Once I showed an attitude of gratitude God would give me a larger space. The Bible said in everything give thanks. I was now going to be thankful for that journey, for the pain for those agonizing nights, God I am thankful. If I did not get in trouble, I wouldn't know how great God is.

I had to stop whining and complaining about what I don't have and start rejoicing and praising God for what I do have. I am not homeless nor hopeless. The basement was small, but my kids were not in a shelter or on the streets. God was showing me that I had to take care of the basement, then *He* would bring me out. Lord, I am grateful and thankful for the basement. I am also thankful to the Lord for where He brought me from, and I trust and believe where *He* was going to take me. Where are you Debbie, God wanted to know? I humbly said here I am Lord. God knew where I was mentally, spiritually, and physically and only *He* could save me.

I must admit, it was rough. I joyfully gave God thanks for the year that passed. I danced in that basement like I was not wearing any shoes. Yes, I did dance like King David. It was truly a year of adversities. As tough as the year was, God brought me through. I am no longer desperate, I have hope. My dance is a dance of praise.

(Psalm 149:3) Let them praise his name in the dance: let them sing praise unto him with the timbrel and harp.

(Psalm 145:2) Every day will I bless thee; and I will praise thy name forever and ever.

(Lamentations 3:22-24) It is of the Lord's mercies that we are not consumed, because his compassions fail not; They are new every morning: great is thy faithfulness' The Lord is my portions, saith my soul; therefore will I hope in him; Verse 25; The LORD is good unto them that wait for him, to the soul that seeketh him.

PHOTO GALLERY

Christmas in the
basement with Debbie
and Mammy Merle.

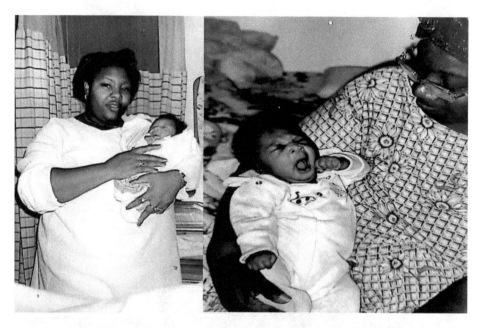

Prudy came from Canada for baby Diamond's birth.
Mammy Merle taking care of Diamond.

Learning to smile in the Basement.

CHAPTER 10

Homeowner

The year 1999 was turning out to be the year of Exodus for me. The house was almost ready. There were a few hurdles to get over. I knew it was not going to be easy. One gigantic hurdle was a dispute with the builders. The final touches on the house stopped. This was no fault of mine, but it worked out beautifully in the end.

Yet again, God showed me he would work it out for my good, just be still and trust *Him*. We would have to wait another two months before the new builders resumed working again. That interruption gave me time to gather up more money to close the deal. Ain't that just like God to just stop everything, so *His* wandering sheep Debbie could catch up with her closing cost payment. He just made a way in the wilderness. With every adversity, and hardship God made a way for me.

> *(Psalm 138:8) The Lord will perfect that which concerneth me: thy mercy, O LORD, endureth forever: forsake not the works of thine own hands.*

The builders finally got things smooth out and The Saratoga Seven Houses were finally done. It was time to close on my house. When I met the lawyer in Manhattan I was not alone, I strongly believe that God and my mother were in that office with me. There was a sense of peace I can't explain. It was as if God had said "Debbie *PEACE BE STILL*." As I sat in that big office the scripture that came back to me was of humility. I must humble myself before the Lord. With all that I have been through, the LORD was saying to me to humble myself and be still and *He* would take care of the rest.

> *(James 4: 6 & 10) But he giveth more grace. Wherefore he saith, God resisteth the proud, but giveth grace unto*

the humble. Humble yourself in the sight of the Lord, and he shall lift you up;

I thank God for the journey. The discipline and the wisdom to hold on and be strong even in adversity. After the signing of the documents the lawyer said something that was so profound. He said "when you walked out of here today you will be a homeowner. Not just a homeowner but also a landlord." Now look at me, Debbie a homeowner. You can't imagine the feeling I had when I thought about the reality of living in the basement and then moving into my own house. Where did you ever hear that? Only God.

I understood that God was in control. This solidifies what it means for God to place you in a large place. The children finally got their own house with their own room. When it was time to move in, I decided to leave everything behind in the basement. No bad memories, everything was staying. We were taking just the clothes on our backs and moving into our own home. I was walking out of the basement with my head held high and my three children in tow. God will provide.

(Isaiah 1:19) If ye be willing and obedient, ye shall eat the good of the land.

I called everyone I knew and offered to give away everything. They could pick and choose whatever they wanted. That feeling was bittersweet no more Ludlum Place. Our brand new house awaits us, new carpet, new appliances, it was amazing. This was truly one of the highlights of my life. We came through the front door with garbage bags of clothes. There were smiles from the children but tears and vindication for me.

(Psalms 126:5) They that sow in tears shall reap in joy.

Our first Thanksgiving we broke bread on the floor. We had no furniture, but we had a home. God, I thank you. With a new house came new responsibilities. I was determined not to lose my home. The baby went into daycare. The children started school and our journey began in our new home. As I reflect on my life, I can say this decision was a monumental decision. I no longer felt like I let down my children. Yes, this was all for them, I just could not raise my children in a basement. I had to show them you could strive for more. It is not where you start but it is where you finish. I will never forget the basement. It taught me how to fight and push for what I wanted. Humility, persistence, and perseverance is how I describe that years' experience. I endured hardship and rejection, but God allowed me to persevere. In some ways the basement really made me a better human being. I will never take for granted what God has done for me. He has done a new thing in my life.

> *(Isaiah 43:19) Behold, I will do a new thing; now it shall spring forth; shall ye not know it? I will even make a way in the wilderness, and rivers in the desert.*

As a child of God, I had a legal right to be happy and live in abundance. It is a gift from God. My mother returned to the US, this time to our new home. My mother was genuinely happy for me and the children. All her prayers paid off. Give God Glory. I spared no expense. I took abundant living to the next level. I drove a brand new Expedition, (Eddie Bauer Edition) out of the show room at the car dealership. We were living the life or so we thought. I was literally spending way more than I should. I just thought that we deserved it. I felt I was deprived for so long that I was treating myself to everything and I mean everything.

I never realized I was way over my head. I really didn't know the logistics of a homeownership and the responsibilities that came with it. I thought I had a house and that meant I had money. I took out an equity line of credit not knowing the real meaning of the word. I just thought that having the house meant I was entitled to that type of cash. No one explained the repercussions of borrowing that large amount of money. Before I knew it, I was struggling to pay back the equity line of credit, the payment on the brand new truck and my college tuition. I wish I had someone to sit me down and literally school me on credit and credit card debt. This horrible chapter in my life was one of my own doing.

I am never going to blame anyone for where I ended up. I heard about the roaring 90s, but now I'm living in the big 2000s. Everything had to be big. I believe I had a big house, so I needed to have a big truck in the driveway. I literally spiraled out of control, financially. For the next five years I fought my way out of that financial basement. Yes, I said it, mentally I felt like I was back in the basement all over again. A hole with no way of getting out. Thank God my mother was here once more. Yet again she was my rock to lean on. She advised me to cut costs and just stop spending. Could you imagine a woman with limited education advising me on economics? She scolded me and said "Debbie, band your belly and live within your means." I took her stern advice and just stopped.

I felt so embarrassed I didn't want anyone to know I was not rich. It took me years to realize that being rich is really a state of mind. Having a big house and a big car doesn't make you rich. I had to get back to being grounded. I first had to realize I had a spending problem and get rid of the credit card. I consolidated everything and had to refinance the house so early in the game. I had to get rid of the truck and cut my losses. Back on foot with no vehicle was my new normal. That was certainly a dark day for me. This is an example of poor judgment and not being educated on credit cards or its pitfalls. I knew there were pros and cons for credit cards, but back then I had no clue how deep in debt you could get if you are not credit smart. I didn't check into any type of rehab for my spending habit, nor did I seek counseling. I just stopped spending. I asked God to free me from the clutches of the spending addiction, and it was an addiction. To God be the glory, *He* did lt.

Sometimes God wants us to just ask, and *He* is always waiting with *His* outstretched hands to help us. When it was all said and done, I cut up all my credit cards, and kept my secret. No more shopping and cruising for me. I had to re-group. God's will for me was not to be drowning in debt. *He* promised to bless me, and I trust *Him.* I was convinced *that He* will deliver me out of my financial woes and keep me focused on *His* word and *His* will for me.

> *(Deuteronomy 28:8) The LORD shall command a blessing upon thee in thy storehouse, and in all that thou settest thine hand unto; and he shall bless thee in the land which the LORD thy God giveth thee.*

As graduation day approached, I had an enormous amount of graduation responsibilities and expenses. This momentous occasion meant momentous spending. I was certainly being tested but I was laser focused and remained committed to the task. I didn't scale back anything. I was going to be responsible with my spending. This time all cash, absolutely no credit, I have learned my lesson. I intend to manage my spending and become a better person financially. Transit overtime was going to do it for me. I worked both days off to keep up with my graduation responsibilities and was able to pay down on my gold graduation ring. Yes, I am buying a gold ring. I needed my ring to symbolize this historic occasion. I remembered my mother telling me that I should invest in a piece of gold. She said back in the days she kept a gold bracelet which she would usually pawn to provide for us when she fell on tough times. Graduating wasn't just a historic moment; it was a gigantic accomplishment. I paid homage to my mother by using her aquamarine birthstone for my gold ring and kept her legacy in tack.

Graduating meant the world to me and I wanted to go out in style. I wanted my mother to see that I did accomplish my goals and most importantly I persevered in spite of adversities. I left Trinidad pregnant, hopeless, and full of shame and I felt I was a disappointment to her. This absolutely was a redemption day for me, and joyful pride for my mother.

The one person I lived to impress was here to witness me graduating. It was not just me graduating, it was the entire Duncan ancestors graduating. I spared no expense. Get the 14 seat Limo ready.

> *(Psalm 146:5) Happy is he that hath the God of Jacob for his help, whose hope is in the LORD his God.*

PHOTO GALLERY

Debbie is a new Homeowner.

Below:
Celebrating Thanksgiving 1999 on the floor and children eating breakfast on the floor.

Debbie's brand
new truck
"Thinking I'm
Rich".

Giving back at the orphanage to the kids.

CHAPTER 11

Graduation

The gang's all here! My mother, brother and children are all in the limo. I did mention this was the biggest academic accomplishment in my life. This graduation was historic, so I went beyond my limits. I know it's going beyond my limits that got me in trouble before, so I stayed true to my word and paid for everything with cash. However I truly believed I deserved this and was adding all the fringes. I was going to make this a grand and joyous event for everyone.

My mother sacrificed everything to get me to this place in my life. My mother, knowing she couldn't afford it, found a way to send me to private school. My mother knew that education was the key to success. She started a hunger in me to become ambitious. My mother planted the seed of perseverance. She sold ice cream, boiled corn, sugar cake, tamarind balls and sweet bread so I can have a decent education. Back then in the early 1970's it was unheard of for a child from my area to attend private school. Your parents had to have money. I can unequivocally tell you where my mother found the money. Mammy Merle sacrificed. Punishing the limits was what my mother did best. She was an entrepreneur in her own right. She was an entrepreneur before she knew the meaning of the word.

Mammy Merle just didn't send one to private school, she sent two. Prudy, my smaller sister also was given that prestigious opportunity. I had to prove I was not just honored, but grateful. To whom much is given, much is required. The little girl attending Saint Thomas Private School in Trinidad wearing her brown and white uniform was now about to graduate from college. This is indeed a blessing from God. The very first of the family to ever walk across a graduation stage. One of the biggest stages in the United States. The

Stage is Madison Square Garden. This was amazing. Out of this world. Now you can understand why I had to get a limo. I had to arrive in style to Madison Square Garden. My wonderful mother sat across from me in the limo, and she smiled. Her smile said it all.

(1 Corinthians 10:31) Whether therefore ye eat, or drink, or whatsoever ye do, do all to the glory of God.

Without words I knew she was proud of me. She witnessed her daughter graduating from college. It's heartbreaking to know that when she was growing up that some of her peers didn't have opportunities for education. I knew in my heart this was a big accomplishment. I accepted my degree with pride and jubilance, the tears could not stop flowing. Coming to America with my small canvas bag with my few belongings, pregnant, struggling for a green card, dropping in and out of school, struggling to pay tuition, I could go on and on. Making it to this point could only be God.

Daily my life was subjected to challenges and disappointments, and I am now able to preserve and graduate. This proves that you can accomplish anything once you put your mind to it. I fully appreciate the saying once God is on the boat I can't drown. Everyone thought that this degree was my PhD, the way I was behaving. I had to proudly announce that this was my Associate Degree in Human Services. If you know me and my journey you will cry for me. This degree was going to pave the way for the children and others that will follow. It was worth the effort to get my family there, even if it meant we had to put the wheelchair in two seats of the limo. My mother had a legal right to witness this and be a part of it. Mammy Merle's health was declining, so I was thankful that my one true role model was able to witness this grand affair. This degree was literally for her and for all her generation who were deprived in some way of a decent education. For me attending college was a generational game changer. I knew I was turning a new page in our family's history books. I hope others that follow could continue the Duncan legacy of working hard and striving for a college education.

As I reflect on all the challenges, stress and expenses leading up to this occasion, I realize success in life is not going to be easy. You have to put in the work. The late nights and those sometimes tough professors really could bring you to the breaking point. However, I do believe it is the power within that sustains you.

(Philippians 2:13) For it is God which worketh in you both to will and to do of his good pleasure.

I graduated in May 2005. I am not one for patting myself on the back, but I am glad I did it in such an extravagant style and grandeur. The following year my world will come to a crashing end. My beloved mother who was smiling at me in the limo was now dead. I went from unspeakable and absolute joy to unbearable heartbreak and loss.

PHOTO GALLERY

Debbie's graduation day

Debbie stepping
out of the limo on
graduation day.

Mammy Merle
smiling at Debbie
in the limo.

CHAPTER 12

Mammy Merle Gone

The year had just started. My mom had her regular doctor's visit. She was upbeat because all her tests from her previous visits were normal. Apart from the arthritis that prevented her from walking she was otherwise ok. We were excited so we decided to take a trip to visit Steven, my brother. He bought a new house in Pennsylvania, and we were all eager to see it. I had no classes, so the trip was set. The ride was about four hours, and we were all exhausted when we got to my brother's house. I got help to move my mother upstairs so she can freshen up and change after the long trip. As I lifted her out of the wheelchair and gently placed her on the bed the unthinkable happened. I briefly turned for her undergarments, my mother slipped off the bed and hit her head on the edge of a stereo on the nightstand. In that split second, I couldn't believe what happened.

All these years my mother lived with me, she never fell or even had a scratch. How could this happen? By the time we arrived at York Hospital in PA. my mother went from a bump on the head to massive bleeding on the brain. I was devastated, how could this happen? My intention was for her to have a weekend of fun with her son in his new home. The doctor said there was bleeding on the brain, and she was in a coma. I was heartbroken. My mother was our rock. All her life she took care of us and how in the world could I let this happen. I literally felt like I failed her. The doctor said that she would have to come out of the coma on her own. I made my way to New York, took time off the job and headed back to PA. Dorrie, my brother's girlfriend, stayed with my brother at Mammy Merle's bedside until I returned. We prayed fervently for Mammy Merle to pull through. Those days at her bedside seemed endless. Father, if there was ever a time that I needed you Lord, it is now.

We earnestly prayed for my mother's recovery, but it didn't happen. Our mother's condition began to worsen, and she was dying. We discussed even moving her back to New York if it would increase her chances of survival. We were desperate. I prayed and told God that Mammy Merle needed *Him*. She was now placed on life-support. As the days passed it was evident that Mammy Merle was brain dead and being kept alive by a machine. It broke our hearts when we saw our mother in that dyer condition.

Steven and I knew we could not let her continue to suffer like that. On January 21, 2006, with considerable advice from the doctors we sorrowfully removed Mammy Merle from the life support machine. I blame myself for taking her to PA, and not having the right medical facility for her. My responsibility was to care for my mother and keep her safe and I failed. My home in New York was fall proof and accommodated her every move. My mother had her own apartment on the first floor in my new house. We installed a ramp for wheelchair access and mobility, she had a home attendant for quality care. I took her out from that safe environment and now she is dead. I was numb and didn't know where to turn. My world was shattered without any warning. I didn't know what to do. I felt like I was in a bad dream that I couldn't wake up from. God where are you? The fact that Mammy Merle lived with me for all those years and never had one incident weigh heavily on my mind. What was I thinking? In essence I was responsible for her care and wellbeing. Every night my lunch break would be spent assisting my mother. I had a thirty-minute lunch break and would gingerly walk or sometimes run to my home and check on my mother. I made sure she was dry, comfortable, and tucked in bed. Her medical bed rails were checked, and I would return to work all in thirty minutes. That was done at 2:30 a.m. every morning.

The depth of my love for her goes all the way back to when she would sacrifice herself for her children. I feel especially in debt to my mother for the foundation she laid for me. I still have fond memories of my mother who taught me how to play cards, she took us to Carnival, she made sure we had clothes if that meant she would be without. She made sure we all had an education. I filed for Mammy Merle to become a US citizen and when she was able to travel to the United States it meant the world to me. Her swearing in ceremony

152

was another big accomplishment. It was my mother that guided me to the Lord. I can recall when I was in my mid teenage years when Mammy Merle went from staunch Catholic to Spiritual Baptist. I didn't think anything of it. I saw it as the same God, just a different house of worship. As the years passed, she became more passionate and worked tirelessly in the church. Mammy Merle simply loved God and lived to worship *Him*. She said the most important thing is maintaining a relationship with *Him*, by loving *Him* with all your heart, with all your soul and with all your mind. It was a joy being in her presence.

(Mathew 22:37) Jesus said unto him, Thou shalt love the Lord thy God with all thy heart, and with all thy soul, and with all thy mind.

There was something about my mother that made me feel golden. When we went out in New York City my mother just had to smile and flash her gold teeth and we were treated like celebrities. I loved pushing her in her wheelchair. We got special treatment everywhere we went. I felt loved and protected in her presence. She was just amazing.

(Proverbs 31:10, 16, 20, 27 & 28) Who can find a virtuous woman? for her price is far above rubies; She considereth a field, and buyeth it: with the fruit of her hands she planteth a vineyard; She stretcheth out her hand to the poor; yea, she reacheth forth her hands to the needy; She looketh well to the ways of her household, and eateth not the bread of idleness; Her children arise up, and call her blessed; her husband also, and he praiseth her.

My mother taught me life skills. Everything I learned contributed to my survival in New York for 19 years. She instilled in me work ethics, perseverance, and strength. Her tenacity was one of the traits that made her special. Now I had to arrange for her body to be brought back to New York. Father God all I ask for is *your* strength. Help our family Lord so we can get through this devastating time. Plans were made for a celebration of life service in New York. After the service her body would be flown to Trinidad, the land of her birth. Once the arrangements were made, I had to get myself and the children to Trinidad.

If you ever had to bury your mother, you know it is one of the hardest things to do. Landing in Trinidad under these conditions was heart wrenching. My oldest brother Anthony was my shoulder to lean on. We were able to have the funeral service at the Cathedral in Port of Spain. I Thank God for the powers that be at the orphanage in Belmont. They were willing to help in any way they could, and their kindness made a stressful situation bearable.

It seemed to be divine intervention if you ask me, because my mother started out in the Catholic faith years ago, and that's where she was eulogized at the home going service. Give God Glory. It doesn't matter your religious belief, Spiritual Baptist or Catholicism, we serve one true God. That was the most memorable moment that came out of my mother's funeral. My mother, my queen, my role model, my friend, my motivator, and my true warrior. Mammy Merle was laid to rest on January 31, 2006.

(1 Thessalonians 4:14) For if we believe that Jesus died and rose again, even so them also which sleep in Jesus will God bring with him.

Caring for my mother was an amazing privilege. I thank God that I was allowed the opportunity to be a loving and caring daughter to her. God allowed me to pay back all the time she took care of me with no charge. I wanted to thank her immensely for getting me this far. Coming back on the plane to New York I felt shattered and so alone. My life was literally drained from me. For the months that followed I would constantly question my actions. Overwhelming guilt forced me into seclusion. I tried to find peace with my mother's death, however I could not shake that cloud of grief that followed me. Daily I became consumed with guilt and unimaginable pain for my mother.

My sorrow was unbearable. Thanks to the comforting presence of the Lord, I was fortunate to find my way. No more self-pity. *He* is a loving and forgiving God. With *His* forgiveness my self-confidence returned. *He* was my light in the darkness. My healing process began with me first forgiving myself and slowly God began to restore my peace. I was able to make it through the grieving process only by God's grace and *His* mercies. It took some time, but God made a way in the wilderness. I have the assurance that Mammy Merle is looking down on me. I thank God that *He* blessed us with a wonderful human being that was my mother. I am forever grateful for the time that God placed her on the earth. It was amazing that everyone was able to celebrate Mammy's life and faith and I was thankful for that. Mammy Merle left us with precious memories of giving and helping others. I hope I could live up to her standards and continue her legacy. I miss her immensely, but I know she is rejoicing in the presence of the LORD free of pain and machines. All my love to you Mammy Merle as you transcend from earth to glory. Rest In Peace.

> *(Proverbs 31:30) Favour is deceitful, and beauty is vain; but a woman that feareth LORD, she shall be praised.*

PHOTO GALLERY

Debbie out with Mammy Merle and having fun.

Mammy Merle's Funeral

CHAPTER 13

MR. & MRS. WHYTE

Working my way back to the classroom was going to be tough because the one person I lived to impress was gone. I felt tired and uninspired, but I was determined to finish and not just finish but finish strong. I was going to dedicate my degree to my mother. The thought of her always being there for me made this degree the motivation for me to push forward when I began falling behind. I have to admit I struggled tremendously, but I was determined to see her smile at me, even if the smile was from heaven.

It was mid 2006 when I ran into an old friend, Mr. Whyte. He was sympathetic to my mother's death, and he became a good listener. He reminded me of his many attempts to meet my mother a while back, but I wouldn't let him. I'm so sorry for that. This was one of my many regrets, because he would end up being my husband. Mr. Whyte never left my side since we reunited. It seemed that Mammy Merle knew I needed someone to physically prop me up. So, she sent a farmer. This was not just any farmer; this was a farmer from the hills of Jamaica. I now realize my mom sent him not just to comfort me but to literally watch my back. I knew I was not ready for a relationship, and he understood that. However, he remained my shoulder to lean on.

I am truly convinced Mr. Whyte was a gift from my mother. Mammy was telling me from above that she could not be there to help me anymore, so she was sending a substitute. As time went by, he became my go to person for everything. I was employed for ten years at MTA, and there was a sense of job security. Now I had to seriously consider the security in my personal life, and Mr. Whyte certainly was the man for the job. Mr. Whyte was a kindhearted and a modest individual.

He loved boasting about growing up in the country parts of Westmoreland in Jamaica with his grandmother and grandfather. He relished farming and shared stories of his humble beginnings of raising goats, cows, and taking his donkey whose name was (hot rod) to the market.

I would be on the floor holding my belly with laughter when he told me how the donkey would run away, and he had to recapture him. We had nothing in common, we were the total opposite. Yet I was smitten by him. I was a town girl from Laventille. The bright lights of Port-of-Spain, Trinidad. I was infatuated by his stories of animal rearing. The closest I came to animals in Trinidad was the chickens in the yard. We knew not to get attached because they were always our Sunday dinner. Yard fowl was what they were called in Trinidad. It made the best stew chicken. I remembered my brother had some pigeons and they too were eaten usually for fun, that was it.

Mr. Whyte was so humble and easygoing; he was a breath of fresh air. Mr. Whyte said his grandmother taught him about Jesus. He would often sing to me his favorite hymn

"I am under the rock; the rock is higher than I. Jehovah hides me. I am under the rock". We very much enjoyed each other's company. I knew I wanted to be his wife and he knew he wanted to be my husband. It was that simple. We both came to the conclusion that we were not going to play games, we were in for the long hall. We knew what we wanted, and we went for it. We compromised on every decision from then on. So, we agreed to have our engagement in Jamaica and be married in Trinidad and Tobago. By the next year 2007 we were in Jamaica getting engaged at the infamous Dons River Falls. We planned the wedding during that year, and it was settled, a destination wedding.

After everything I had to deal with, I longed for a happy place. We picked Tobago's renowned Coco Reef Resort and Spa. It was a white affair. Everyone wore white and we wore ivory. It was a wedding for the ages. Destination weddings really are the way to go. The ambience, the sandy beach, the food! Everything is literally done for you. All you do is pick the color scheme and the menu and show up.

On that beautiful day in May 2008, we were married. It was an amazing wedding, we did it in style. My husband, his parents, and his son, myself and my children except Latonya and the New York guest flew in together. It was unforgettable. The Trinidad guest was treated to an extraordinary time at the CoCo Reef Resort. It really lived up to its name. The bridal party went snorkeling with the fish. They also were treated with a wonderful adventure in the ocean on the famous glass bottom boat. Sometimes it really pays to dream big and step out on your dreams.

> *(Ecclesiastes 3:13) And also that every man should eat and drink, and enjoy the good of all his labour, it is the gift of God.*

We reconnected, we married, and we were going to make our own plans for our future. This was one of the first decisions we made together, and we can truly say we nailed it. I am now a married woman. It does feel good. The hospitality at the hotel was so wonderful so we decided to stay another week. I knew once we returned to New York our work schedule would be rough, so we enjoyed every bit of time on the beach.

We had a beautiful wedding and a wonderful time in Tobago. It was then reality set in that the honeymoon was over. We had to leave Tobago, but we are now leaving as one flesh.

> *(Genesis 2:24) Therefore shall a man leave his father and his mother and shall cleave unto his wife: and they shall be one flesh.*

Back in New York I was ready to begin my new life as a married woman. I was happy to have someone on my side who was genuinely in my corner. I didn't have to work as hard anymore, and it felt wonderful. I had a partner that was behind me one hundred percent and I had help financially and emotionally. Now I can finish what I started years ago and be in full pursuit of my Bachelor's degree. I could register for more classes and not feel like I am financially drowning. I went hard towards my goal and registered for five classes. By the next year 2009 I was on my way to getting my degree. In the end I was mentally drained but I did it. Some days it was challenging, but I managed to stay focused and I made it through. As I promised, my degree was dedicated to Mammy Merle.

I had to return in 2010 for one more class but I was fine with that. I now was officially done with college. The immigrant girl, cleaning houses, selling KFC chicken, living in a basement is finally graduating college. It took almost twenty years of blood sweat and tears, but I graduated with a Bachelor's degree in Human Services. Mammy Merle was not here to witness this wonderful achievement, but to God I give the glory and to her I dedicate my degree. The road traveled for my degree reflects Mammy Merle, hard work, perseverance, and sheer determination. I wanted to be grateful to all the friends and family who encouraged and supported me. This degree solidifies my journey. We all can start something, but it takes grit, stamina, and dedication to finish it.

(Psalm 94:17) Unless the Lord had been my help, my soul had almost dwelt in silence.

God is doing a new thing in my life, so I made an oath that the next book I was going to focus on and never put down was my bible, and so it was. I enrolled in the Freedom Hall Bible Institute. I wanted to get more knowledge of the Bible. I yearned for a clear understanding of my existence and my purpose in the world. My deepest desire is to know more about my savior, and why he kept loving me, providing for me even when I was not deserving of *His* love. The truth be told, I wholeheartedly wanted to hook up with and be closer to The Lord and Savior Jesus Christ.

PHOTO GALLERY

Mr. & Mrs. Whyte
Engagement in
Don River Falls in
Jamaica

Mr. & Mrs. Whyte
wedding in Tobago

CHAPTER 14

NO CROSS NO CROWN

The bible school shared the importance of developing and maintaining a relationship with the Lord by daily prayer and meditation. I always knew if you love someone your desire is to spend every breath of your day with that individual. So, for years I would write letters to the Lord in the form of my journal entry, but now there was a difference. I had an inner sense of purpose. As I reignited my relationship with *Him,* my journal entries now became love letters. This daily discipline bolstered my relationship with the LORD. I had a renewed confidence in *His* presence, and *His* constant love for me. I worked hard to foster this relationship and I credit my love letters to the LORD for keeping me passionate and unwavering in my spiritual walk of faith. My hunger and thirst for the Lord was evident. With a joyful heart I accepted *His* transforming presence.

> *(Psalm 34:8) O taste and see that the Lord is good: blessed is the man that trusteth in him.*

My understanding was instant. It's like a light bulb that was dim became illuminated. The book itself was so intriguing I could not lay it down. The bible covered everything such as, war, crime, murders, adultery, betrayal, bribery, deception, treachery, jealousy, trickery, theft, love, hate, victory, defeat, redemption and so much more. The bible opened my eyes to the world around me. For me it was my road map and initially became my compass for my life and my way of living. When you begin to know the Lord and believe in *His* word you become strong and empowered.

I realized I had to stay close to the Lord if I wanted to really know *Him*. I wanted to be a better person spiritually and the only way to accomplish that was by walking hand in hand with the Lord. Daily I yearn for a more intimate relationship with the LORD and what I got in return was life altering. I essentially became a changed human being. My deep dive into the word enlightened me and the longer I stayed in the word the stronger I became. My desire is to live my best life for the *LORD*.

The bible school was one of the best decisions I have made in my spiritual life. Learning to walk with the LORD required adjustment. I had to examine myself. My quest to be in *His* presence forced me to do inventory with my entire life. My desire is not to just survive, it is to thrive holistically in mind, body, and soul.

I began inventory on every aspect of my life. I had to start calculating my financial future and also retirement. My husband and I decided to do some investments. We first started with Trinidad. I acquired a small piece of property from Sharon's Mother, Miss Nita. We decided that would be great as a retirement property. It will take another year before we start building but we were focused on maintaining our own accommodations in Trinidad.

(Proverbs 19:8) He that getteth wisdom loveth his own soul: he that keepeth understanding shall find good.

While I am busy getting my retirement home ready and setting up my future plans, my son Anthony (aka G.I. Joe) was also getting busy. Anthony had a baby on the way. I was soon to be a grandmother, yes Debbie a grandmother. My beautiful Serenity was born November 2012 in the height of President Obama's re-election. What a gift. He remained in the White House, and I got a granddaughter to love and cherish. All around it was a win-win situation in 2012.

Sixteen years in transit just flew bye. Lord, where does the time go? I just have 10 years left to get my finances in order, before you know it, retirement is upon me. In 2015 Diamond will be going off to college and that was just three years away. I kept my focus and stayed true to my word. In 2013 I graduated with a bachelors in theology from Freedom Hall Bible Institute. I was the Salutatorian in our graduating class. I did say I was not going to lay down my Bible, right? I never looked at another book. I remained focused and completed my goals. Graduating from the bible school was bittersweet for me, my mom was not here but she was instrumental in leading me on a path that brought me to the *LORD*.

I kept up the pace after graduation and continued to push for Diamond to make her way to the college gate. I didn't want to shortchange her dreams of an HBCU education. So, I pressed on the overtime gas full steam ahead. I had to admit this was a grueling year of work, but God never left me. He was really on my side. It's always when you are doing well the enemy shows up his ugly head, and in this case, it was in the form of a bad tenant. If you ever had a bad tenant like the one, I am referring to you will empathize with me. I literally got a bald spot from all the courtroom appearances.

Imagine graduating from the Bible school feeling strong and empowered, then the enemy pops up their ugly head. It reminded me of when Jesus came down from the mountain after fasting for forty days and forty nights. The very first person he met was the devil. This is a friendly reminder; the enemy doesn't care if you are in the Bible school or not. The Bible says, the enemy comes to kill, steal, and destroy but *He* came that we might have life and have it more abundantly. You have to always be on guard to resist the enemy and his devices. I thank God for *His* strength to get them out.

The LORD gave us the power to step on scorpions. When it was all said and done, they were out. I had a bald spot from stress, but God kept me. I dealt with them the only way I knew how. With my trusty Bible and the true word of God. Every day I was on my knees and God heard my cry. Two Thousand and Fourteen showed me again that God is going to fight my battle and he did. He cut off the enemy's head completely and they were gone from my property. In the name of Jesus. No more courtroom drama. I conquered that mountain and now I can focus on conquering another, and that is ushering Diamond off to college.

(Exodus 14:14) The Lord shall fight for you, and you shall hold your peace.

PHOTO GALLERY

New Grandbaby

Graduating from Bible School

CHAPTER 15

HBCU

Diamond's HBCU dreams came true. I was happy for her when she received her acceptance letter. She was heading to Clark Atlanta University. She dared to dream and now it has become a reality. This is a testament of God's love and faithfulness towards her. She learned her very first lesson in perseverance before she even entered college. I honestly wanted Spelman College, but this is not my dream it was hers. When you desire something bad enough you work hard for it, and that she did. Diamond knew what she wanted since the tenth grade, and she pushed herself. Her road to the college door was compared to climbing a mountain; high and unattainable. She didn't run from the mountain she began to climb. Her ambitions heightened when she visited several colleges in the South. I am glad I approved that college trip because it piqued her curiosity even more for HBCU experience. When she returned, she began taking Saturday classes to enhance her college preparedness. Diamond realized that some mountains are challenging and most times for fear of failure, there is an unwillingness to even attempt the climb, but not her. Her expectations were high, and the wait was unnerving, but she persevered in the end. We knew that this was a momentous occasion in our family. Dropping her off that day was indescribable.

An immigrant that came to the United States with $85 to her name, is now registering her American born daughter in an Historically Black College in the south. It was an amazing day for my entire family. Our ancestors were clapping their hands and jumping for joy. The ones that broke their backs on the plantations were singing psalms and doing a praise dance. It was indeed a time for rejoicing and I owe it all to God. I am not just giddy, I am elated. I was bursting with pride and grateful for how far we have come. For some, a college education often seems out of reach. I am honored and extremely blessed that I am able to support Diamond financially in her journey. In some countries it is so difficult for young people, especially girls, to get an education. The tears began to flow. It shows hard work really does pay off.

> *(Psalm 37: 4-5) Delight thyself also in the LORD; and he shall give thee the desires of thine heart; Commit thy way unto the LORD; trust also in him; and he shall bring it to pass.*

My husband and I packed her up and she was off to her dream school Clark Atlanta University. She didn't have to worry; I had The Almighty God and MTA to get us through. I must tell you, some days it was dicey, but God made a way in the wilderness. I worked six days a week and stayed focused. I know firsthand how the college experience could be without adequate finances. I was definitely going to support Diamond with any and all resources at my disposal. I was excited about walking with Diamond through her incredible journey. I was a proud mother of a child in college, not just any college, Clark

Atlanta University. I know the power of education and I was proud to endorse that power.

The first semester went by pretty quick, we both breathed a sigh of relief; however, the real work began once she got deeper into her major. I began to relax when she had two semesters wrapped up. Only God knew how she would return for the following semesters. I just had to wait for *Him* to lead the way. My God came through again for us, this one came out of nowhere, it literally was jaw dropping. In 2016 we got a windfall, back child support. Could you imagine, this could only be God.

A note to all those parents out there. Please provide for your children. It's your duty as a parent. Giving support to your child is the responsible thing to do. The back child support payment we received filled in for the next two semesters. It was that much. I thank God for the well needed blessings. That windfall kept us afloat. Thank God. Clark Atlanta University's saying is "FIND A WAY OR MAKE ONE."

I tapped into my 401k for the 2017 semesters. I was pulling money from everywhere. Any resource that presented itself was going to be utilized. I was wiring money left and right. She was going to college on prayer and adrenaline. Diamond landed a Resident Assistant job on campus that helped a whole lot. It was all hands on deck. Daily my husband and I were juggling to keep things afloat. By the time 2018 came around I was running on empty. We were almost to the finish line. I was actually seeing the light at the end of the tunnel. With all the excitement I didn't notice I was putting on weight. I knew I was working hard, hustling overtime, and not eating right. My husband was doing most of the cooking so I would often indulge in his Jamaican dumplings. I also was not managing my blood pressure. I am thinking I can do this. I never thought my body would give out on me. However, it did.

PHOTO GALLERY

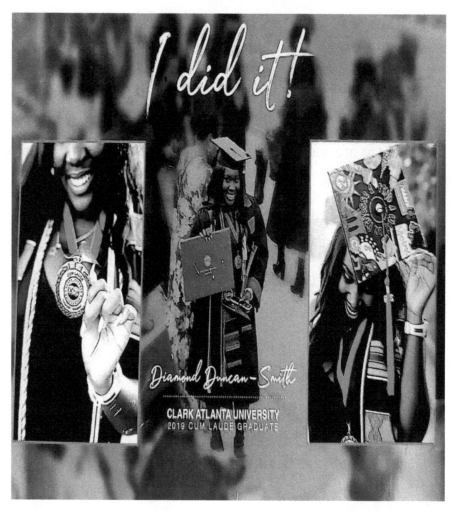

My daughter Diamond's HBCU Graduation.

CHAPTER 16

Second Chance

One Sunday morning while getting ready for church. I felt a sharp pain in my chest, I brushed it off as heartburn. Within minutes I was feeling hot and was sweating profusely. I called my husband who had already left for his weekend job and told him what was happening. He told me he was leaving the job and he was on his way home. Latonya had already gone to the gym, so I am alone. Unknowing to me, I was having a heart attack (myocardial infarction). To my knowledge, I didn't have any history of heart disease in my family. A heart attack was the farthest thing from my mind, I am still thinking this is heartburn.

I was only on medication for high blood pressure, nothing more. I managed to call 911 when I realized the pain was increasing. This was not heartburn, clearly something was wrong. Within minutes the ambulance arrived. As I entered the ambulance I began throwing up. I was rushed to the hospital stricken with pain, fear, and uncertainty. I credit the EMT, and their rapid response for saving my life. At the hospital the pain was too much to bear. I remembered the doctor at the emergency room moving very quickly around my bed as I drifted off with an oxygen mask on my face. Again, God was on my side.

> *(Psalm 124: 1-2) If it had not been the LORD who was on our side, now may Israel say; If it had not been the LORD who was on our side, when men rose up against us.*

Imagine me having a heart attack. To all the women that wear so many hats as a wife, mother, aunty, niece, and grandmother, we have to take care of our health. We are caregivers to everyone, and most times we neglect our own health. As women we do everything. We are home makers in every sense of the word. We cook, clean, and then do homework with children. We are in a board meeting, PTA meeting, church meeting. Making doctors' appointments, usually never for ourselves, we do it all. Our sleeping hours are usually not the doctor recommended amount. Our schedules are often overwhelming, and we end up being overworked, frustrated, and stressed and in my case contributed to heart issues.

The doctors performed the procedure called Coronary angioplasty. I came out of surgery grateful to be alive with a new lease on life. God gave me another chance to get my life right and maintain a healthy lifestyle. After what I have experienced, I am committed to living and enjoying a healthier life. I had to monitor my cholesterol and stay away from greasy foods and go easy on the Jamaican dumplings. Long story short, I am now living to praise God and eat healthy. It was a rocky road to recovery, but I am still standing.

> *(Psalm 118:17) I shall not die but live and declare the works of the Lord.*

> *(Psalm 69:30) I will praise the name of the God with a song, and will magnify him with thanksgiving.*

I would not forget the Doctors and nurses that saved my life at Downstate Medical Hospital. I thank God for guiding their hands as they worked to save my life and prove again *His* *un*conditional love towards me. My older daughter Latonya was in charge of my diet. I must admit change is good. I thank God that *He had* sent her back home months earlier, now we knew it was to help me in my recovery. She helped my heart heal in more ways than one. Sometimes we wonder why things happen, however I learned a long time ago that I am allowed to ask God questions, but I am not allowed to question God. This is the daughter that I fought so hard to get out of Trinidad and years later she is helping with my health care plan. God you are indeed a miracle working God.

It was only by God's grace that I was well enough the next year to witness Diamond walk across the stage at Clark Atlanta University. I am thankful to God that I was given the opportunity to see her accomplish her dreams. God is awesome, *He* kept me alive for a reason and a purpose. Diamond didn't just graduate; she took it to the next level. I knew generational curses were broken that day. She went a step further up the ladder. Diamond graduated Cum Laude. I am genuinely proud of her and so are our ancestors.

I pray daily for Diamond to live out her purpose and be a positive change in the world. The same way my mother paved the way for me. Today with her accomplishment, Diamond can pave the way for another Duncan, and continue our rich heritage of perseverance and determination.

For the year 2019 I was going to have a positive outlook on life. I was serious about my health. I stayed on my daughter's strict diet, and I continued my meditation regimen and tried to limit any stressors. This new lifestyle worked out as a plus for me, I was eating healthy and shedding some unwanted pounds at the same time. I have been home for almost five months, and I am thankful to God for saving me. Although I was out of work for that many months God was indeed our provider.

He provided for us and strengthened my husband as he held us down until I was able to get back on my feet. I am ever grateful that we were fortunate in keeping up with our monthly financial commitments and living expenses. With God's grace we never fell behind and that was a testament to

His goodness towards us. *His* promise was never to leave me nor forsake me. My husband kept up the pace and remained resolved. When I returned to work, I was grateful to God for being my provider. It was only because of *His* grace and mercies we never faltered. I knew I had to find a way to give God thanks for bringing me through to the other side. So, I continued to pray daily for *His* guidance and wisdom for my next step.

> *(Psalm 25:4-5) Shew me thy ways, O LORD; teach me thy paths. Lead me in thy truth, and teach me: for thou art the God of my salvation; on thee do I wait all the day.*

> *(Psalm 27:8) When thou saidst, Seek ye my face; my heart said unto thee, Thy face, LORD, will I seek.*

CHAPTER 17

OVERFLOW

One day after meditation, I saw the tubs of clothes sitting in the corner of my bedroom. They were the result of my closet overflowing. God was so good to me that I was living in the overflow. I couldn't believe it. My closet was so full that I had to store clothes in tubs. Then it came to me. Give it all away. God, you did it again. The Heavenly Father instructed me to bless others with the overflow. I was going to my closet with a plan to give away the overflow. I told my husband what God had placed in my heart and he was on board. He also was guilty of having too much and not doing anything about it. We were able to pack four barrels just from both of our closets.

We went a step further and revealed what God had laid on my heart to others. We told friends, neighbors, and coworkers. We then fill four more barrels with nonperishable food and basic necessities. Our four barrels jumped to a total of twelve with the generous help from others. The outpouring was remarkable. We shipped the barrels to the address in Haiti and notified our contact that the shipment was on the way.

Things were working out in such an awesome way; you knew it had to be God. God just wanted to see how willing and obedient I was. One year to the date of my release from Downstate Medical Hospital. I was on my way to Haiti with my husband on my side. Why did we pick Haiti? Only God knows. As I said earlier, I am allowed to ask God questions, but I am not allowed to question God. He is the one directing my footsteps. I am only going where *He* leads me. I am in awe of how every aspect of this journey worked out. Everything was done in the strength of the Lord, and it was perfect.

(Psalm 138:8) The LORD will perfect that which concerneth me: thy mercy, O LORD endureth for ever: forsake not the works of thine own hand.

We made it to Haiti with absolutely no problem. Our contact on the ground was Avenelle. She was waiting for us with a huge smile on her face at the airport in Port-au-Prince. I initially reached out to Avenelle by phone for assistance some months before the trip, after hearing about the work she was doing in Trinidad and around the Caribbean. I thought she might be the perfect person to work with us. I reached out to her and planned to meet in Trinidad, unfortunately I never got to meet up with her. However, we finally met on a plane flying back from Trinidad to the United States. I told her what God inspired me to do and when the plane landed everything was settled. She provided me with an address for shipping the barrels and promised to help us with whatsoever we needed.

Avenelle also agreed to join us in Haiti. It was amazing. It was as if God had just cleared the way for us to do *His* work. Our transportation, our place to stay, everything was done with such precision. Avenelle had everything prepared and in place for us. I no longer needed to be persuaded, I know God talks to people's hearts. It was nothing short of miraculous. I was marveled at the power of God and what we were able to accomplish. I thank God for allowing me to be obedient. I truly believe *He* will bless you in a place only if *He* sends you to that place. I am convinced *He* was directing our mission.

> *(Isaiah 41:13) For I the LORD thy God will hold thy right hand, saying unto thee, Fear not; I will help thee.*

The yellow school bus was parked at the airport in Port-au-Prince Patiently waiting for us with six barrels. When I asked how and where she got a yellow school bus, she responded by saying not how, *WHO*. Jesus is real. Avenelle had done a lot of humanitarian work in Haiti, so she knew her way around. She was doing her work for the Lord, and it was admirable. I prayed to God for *His* wisdom and thanked *Him* for His guidance. I felt energized and infused with *His* courage and strength. I positioned myself for what God wanted me to do next. I sincerely believe God was orchestrating every detail of this trip. As we landed, we were heading to the orphanage to distribute supplies. We landed on Wednesday, September 11, 2019, and immediately we were on our way in the yellow school bus to the first orphanage in Port-au-Prince. We covered three orphanages before it began to become dark, so we headed to the newly built house Avenelle's Organization (ITNAC) had prepared for us in Haiti. Avenelle suggested that we travel to the countryside the next day. She indicated there would be a greater need in those areas.

Thursday September 12th we were on the tedious journey to the countryside of Haiti. Here I am recovering from a heart attack, and I am in the rough terrain of Haiti. This could only be God. My husband and I grew up only hearing about Haiti. Now we were able to walk and interact with the people of Haiti. With our own eyes we were able to capture firsthand the vastness and beauty of the country. This experience was something I will never forget.

(Micah 6:8) He hath shewed thee, O man, what is good; and what doth the LORD require of thee, but to do justly, and to love mercy, and to walk humbly with God?

Going from village to village and handing out food and clothes gave me a new perspective on life. Lord, was this my purpose? There was a tremendous need in these areas. Avenelle was absolutely right. Some areas don't have running water. We were heartbroken when our barrels went empty, and villagers were turned away. This is Haiti, our Caribbean neighbor. What went wrong? We ran out of food, could you imagine. The only words I could muster, was we will be back. It was a life changing moment for myself and my husband. We had so much food at home in the United States and I am witnessing tremendous lack.

It was right at that exact moment that I realized that I wanted to do this forever. I remembered when my mom was alive, and when we would return to Trinidad, we often visited the Orphanage in Belmont. With the permission from the Administration, we will have a party for the children and distribute toys and clothing. It always brought joy to my heart to see the children so happy. However, this trip was totally different. It was something I could not fathom. How could a country be so rich with resources and yet have so little? I agree more needs to be done. I am praying God will guide and enlighten us on the next step. That trip to Haiti definitely changed my life.

(Ephesians 6:7-8) With good will doing service, as to the Lord, and not to men; Knowing that whatsoever

good thing any man doeth, the same shall he receive of the Lord, whether he be bond or free.

Friday September 13, 2019 was the end of our three day mission. We were traveling back to the United States that day. I thank God for showing me the need and giving me the strength to carry out *His* will. It took me to become incapacitated and locked away in my room to realize my purpose in life. I had to help others. I am grateful to *Him* for giving me a new lease on life. I now have a clear and precise understanding of the saying; *you are not really living if you are not giving.* Those words have been my mantra since I left Haiti. I want to give more, in order to live more. God has truly blessed me, and I want to share it. I just don't want to share food and raiment; I want to share *HIS* word. My only regret was the reading material I took to hand out was written in English and not Creole. I had to let my brothers and sisters in Haiti know that God was a good God in any language. A God of real miracles. *He* was a God that walked with me daily. *He* was there in my darkest moments, and he was there in my triumph. *He* was there through it all.

197

(Mathew 25:40) And the King shall answer and say unto them, Verily I say unto you, Inasmuch as ye have done it unto one of the least of these my brethren, ye have done it unto me.

We were so inspired and transformed by what we saw in Haiti, that we committed ourselves to packing another twelve barrels. The same format, coworkers and neighbors helped once again. One neighbor Cleo donated a seven-drawer dresser slated for one of the orphanages in Port-au-Prince. We had several officers from the Transit District 33 Precinct donate items as well. It was just amazing. Once we told others of our experience in Haiti, they all had a heart to give. We managed to send another 12 barrels and the donated dresser to Haiti. Again, it was an amazing outpouring of love and compassion shown by our neighbors and friends. We plan to return in 2020 to distribute the barrels to the village where we fell short and had promised to return. Also, areas that were in desperate need of resources.

While we are planning our return trip, here comes the dreadful (Covid-19) pandemic. We never knew the severity of this virus until it was directly upon us. New York State was directly in the eye of the pandemic. When we realized how deadly this virus was, we had lost thousands of human lives. A travel ban went into effect, our Haiti plans are now derailed.

Everything stopped and I mean everything. This is my first pandemic in my 56 years on this earth, and like most people I had many questions and concerns. Families couldn't visit their loved ones in the nursing homes and hospitals. Some patients that lost their lives were sadly alone. Loved ones couldn't be there to comfort them. Students had to interact with their teachers and professors virtually from home, known as remote learning. Zoom calls and conferences were the new normal for most businesses and places of worship. The isolation was definitely taking a toll on the nation.

Only essential workers were allowed on the streets and guess who, had an essential job. With an underlying illness, (heart disease) I had to work through the (Covid-19) pandemic, but God was my strong tower. *He* promised to send *His* angels to cover me, and I had to trust *His* word.

(Psalm 91:11) For he shall give his angels charge over thee, to keep thee in all thy ways.

Jesus faced the worst of adversities when *He* walked the earth. *His* Father was with *Him* through it all. I was grateful I was able to work through a raging Pandemic with my Heavenly Father at my side all the way. Shelter in place was the word of the day. The fear that swept through our nation was indescribable. Daily people were dying by the hundreds, without relatives at their side, while first responders were stretched to their limits. Health care workers were taking a beating. They were overworked and stretched to the seams.

Everyday MTA workers had to mask up and report to work and keep the Transportation system working. My health and wellbeing were being tested daily. It was a sad case of events. However, I thank God for holding me tight. The country was engulfed by death and despair, we could only rely on God for his protection and his strength. Even though the pandemic is still raging on, and we are hopeful for the vaccine, believers continue to trust in the word of God and *His* promises towards *His* children. I have been through some rough times in my life, but I realize that God is speaking to me in this season. *He* is the Almighty God. *He* has the power to lift up and put down and *He* is leading me in this wilderness.

> *(Micah 7:7) Therefore I will look unto the LORD; I will wait for the God of my salvation: my God will hear me.*

My son Anthony alluded to the fact that God has been an amazing force in my life. He indeed is THE TRUE and LIVING GOD. Anthony said that I made it through the horrible snowstorm in 1996 that crippled the city. I made it through the World Trade Center bombing in 2001 that claimed thousands of lives. I made it through the blackout in 2003 that stranded thousands in subway tunnels, my little daughter included. I made it through the subway strike in 2005 that affected millions. I made it through Superstorm Sandy in 2012 that devastated thousands. I survived a life changing heart attack in 2018 and I am thankful for another chance of life. I am not naïve. I know life has tragedies and misfortunes but some days I had to wonder what was going on. So many disasters and we were not done yet, I thought hurricane Sandy was disastrous, well here comes hurricane Ida. Hurricane Ida flooded places that had never seen flooding before, including my basement.

After hearing the news, I found out I was blessed to just have water damages from the flooding. Unfortunately, families drowned in their basements in this horrible hurricane. New York had not seen so much water that quickly and our streets and drains couldn't handle it and the result was catastrophic. This horrible event resonated with me because back in the 90's I lived in a basement for years and God protected me and my children from harm. I know when to say thank You JESUS. Just as I am about to breathe a sigh of relief, we were clobbered by a pandemic in 2020. My son was right, through it all God has kept me. I have witnessed and experienced all these challenges and devastations while working in the New York City Subway System and I am still standing. When I consider all, I have been through for all those years and lived to talk about, I can truly proclaim I am extremely blessed. I am grateful to God for bringing me through. I am walking away knowing that I am covered by THE ALMIGHTY GOD. As I evaluate my years in the New

York City Subways and all my adversities and life altering situations, I realize God indeed has been ordering my footsteps. God has a new direction for me to follow and that path is retirement. *He* is God overall and *He* is in charge of my life and wherever *He* leads me I will follow.

(Psalm 73:28) But it is good for me to draw near to God: I have put my trust in the Lord GOD, that I may declare all thy works.

PHOTO GALLERY

Distributing clothes and food in Haiti

Barrels of clothes and food for Haiti

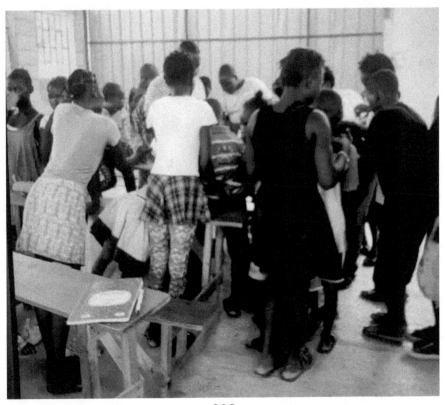

CHAPTER 18

Retirement

As I sat in the booth and reflected on my life, I realized that God has truly blessed me. I am indeed thankful. I am working in the pandemic, and I give God thanks for my safety. Again, I am grateful for *His* miraculous blessing. With God's permission I thanked New York City Transit for my 25 1/2 years of employment services. I am ready for retirement. I discussed my decision with my husband and children and went ahead with God's plans for me. In 2021 I courageously began the retirement proceedings. It seems that the years flew by. I must admit it didn't seem like I worked for that many years. When I reflect on my early days as an employee dragging those buckets of tokens at Grand Central station, at the Time Square Station, Utica Avenue Station, Main Street Flushing; just to name a few and never having been robbed or any other incident, a sense of gratitude flows through me. I am grateful to every transit employee that ever crossed my path, that includes management right on down. I never met a more wonderful group of people in my life. I could not have finished this marathon without their help and support. I would be remiss if I didn't extend my sincere thanks to my customers at my final station of employment, Rockaway Avenue. Once I extended courtesy and care to them, they reciprocated with love and respect, and I would always carry this with me.

I lost some friends and coworkers through the years, and I wanted to say it has been a pleasure knowing them. I want to thank each one for sowing into my life and may their souls rest in peace. I was incredibly blessed to have employment with MTA, and I thank God for all the good fortune I was able to receive as I serve in this company. The journey started at Hopkinson Avenue when I walked through that turnstile in 1987 as a pregnant young woman unsure of my future. Now almost thirty-five years later I am retiring from the same station now called Rockaway Ave. If this is not a Full Circle moment, I don't know what is. This is not an (OMG) moment, it is a (GGG) moment, GIVE GOD GLORY. He brought me through the wilderness and set me in a large place. Father God *you* alone have been my help. I can truly shout *Emmanuel* (God with us.)

> *(Psalm 40:1-3) I waited patiently for the LORD; and he inclined unto me and heard my cry; He brought me up also out of a horrible pit, out of the miry clay, and set my feet upon a rock, and established my goings; And he hath put a new song in my mouth, even praise unto our God: many shall see it, and fear, and shall trust in the LORD.*

I am not going to make any plans, I know better. I humbly submit to God. *He* has my life in *His* hands. I can truly say God has ordered my footsteps. I don't know what the future holds but I do know *who* holds the future. Once God gives me the green light, I will resume activities from where I left off before the pandemic. As I said before *you are not living until you are giving.* I would like to return to Haiti and finish the work that the Lord had started in me. I'm praying to God for health and strength to get us back to that particular village. What the Lord placed in my spirit I pray comes to fruition. I am fully aware of what it means to have *Him* as LORD of my life. I humble myself to you Lord, use me.

> *(Philippians 1:6) Being confident of this very thing, that he which hath begun a good work in you will perform it until the day of Jesus Christ.*

I thank God for *His* guidance every step of the way. I am not ashamed of my journey, On the contrary, I am thankful for it. My trials and adversities have only strengthened my spiritual muscles. I can truly say it was because of *His* grace I am here today. I am able to tell my story without fear. It is refreshing to be open and transparent. I believe when you are your authentic self, God looks within and works on the heart. God cleans you up from the inside out. I believe being fake, disingenuous, and secretive leads to lies and deceptions. This behavior is displeasing to God and *He* is unable to work with me. After all I have been through, I am deeply honored to share my story. This is my story to tell. It cannot be distorted, rewritten, or misinterpreted by anyone because I lived it. I endured the pain, hardship, and rejection. I survived the beat downs and every other adversity that came my way. I worked hard to educate myself and my children while remaining focused on the job. You cannot tell the story if you didn't live it, and it's only by *God's* grace and mercy that I am still standing. I thank God for the confidence to be transparent and honest. In my vulnerability God has favored me. I desperately needed to go to *Him* broken and in pieces so *He can tenderly work with me. He* spent years putting me together while allowing me more time in *His* presence. As *He* is taking *His* precious time working on me, I have realized through the years with my vulnerability and weakness, *He* was indeed my strength.

> *(Isaiah 64:8) But now, O LORD, thou art our father; we are the clay, and thou our potter, and we all are the work of thy hand.*

I am free to cry knowing that God puts *my tears in a bottle*. As the years passed my life experienced hard seasons and valuable lessons. In one season I cleaned homes and sold fried chicken. The lesson learned was humility and thankfulness.

In the next season I sorted mail and sold MetroCards. The lesson learned was sustainability and appreciation. In this season of retirement, I learned contentment, gratitude, and bold faith.

At times in those harsh seasons and stormy days I swore I was going to drown. However, God was always there to still the waters. I am so confident in God's love for me now. I have a built-up assurance, that once Jesus is on the boat, I do not need to know how to swim, nor do I need a life jacket. I am strong in the Lord and in the power of *His* might. I am an overcomer. I fully acknowledge that success doesn't come without a struggle. I couldn't have made it through this journey had it not been for the Lord. Yes, it was a journey of struggles, failures, tragedy and much pain, however God strengthened me and I persevered. I have matured and now understand that suffering builds character. Every one of my adversities had a purpose. It made me stronger. I have come to realize that my most agonizing disappointments served as the catalyst to my unwavering faith and deep trust in God.

(1 Corinthians 15:10) But by the grace of God I am what I am: and his grace which was bestowed upon me

was not in vain; but I laboured more abundantly than they all: yet not I, but the grace of God which was with me.

With growth and maturity, I understand that the storms of life were just that, storms, they came to pass. I weathered the storms and showed resilience and perseverance. After they passed, I thankfully was still standing. I humbly release the pain of the past. It is now behind me. I realize that I couldn't be completely free if I continue to hold onto the past. Give God Glory! Today my joy is renewed, my peace is restored and my relationship with the Lord is strengthened. With God I am able to shine and be the light that *He* required me to be.

(Mathew 5:16) Let your light so shine before men, that they may see your good works, and glorify your Father which is in heaven.

He has smoothed my jagged edges and made me whole again. It was all done in *His* time. I asked at the beginning of my journey if *God* knew me. I found out after all these years *He* walked with me, *He* talked with me, and *He* made me *His* own. I have learned that my life is not my own. God knew me from the womb and guided me through childhood. I will never underestimate the prayer of my Mammy Merle. I am convinced it was her steady stream of prayers that became a hedge around me, ultimately keeping me safe and alive for all those years. God heard her prayers, and *He* protected me. I came to the wonderful conclusion that I am precious to *Him*.

(Romans 5:8) But God commendeth his love toward us, in that while we were yet sinners, Christ died for us.

This journey solidifies God's promises towards me, and *He* kept *His* word. *He* promises to replenish my thirsty soul. Now I yearn to be with *Him,* my love letters are never ending. Now I walk with bold confidence knowing that *He* is walking with me. I understand God's love for me. I conducted my very own experiment: if you stay close to God, *He* will indeed stay close to you. I will advise anyone if you genuinely desire to know God, please stay close to *Him*. My wish is to continue growing in the knowledge of the Lord so I can testify to others of *His* goodness. Even with my inadequacies *He* continues to mold and shape me to what *He* wants me to be. *He* flourished me with his love. I have an assured future because Jesus died and rose again for me.

I will continue to cry out to the Lord because *He* is Sovereign. One of my favorite stories in the bible was about a blind man named Bartimaeus. He desperately tried to get Jesus' attention in a large crowd of people. Jesus was passing through Jericho and Bartimaeus using his boldness and fearlessness cried out to *Him*, others in the crowd who had their sight, selfishly tried to silence him. Bartimaeus cried out even louder and louder and didn't stop until Jesus stopped. Jesus called him and restored his sight.

I am like that man. I cried out to Jesus and even when I was told to shut up, I desperately cried out. Yes, I was blind now I can see. I have learned to cry boldly, bravely, and boisterously in spite of the crowd. I no longer fear what man says, I now know what God says. I am *His* child. *He* calls me friend. Through the years I have learned that man's opinion of me doesn't matter. If you are invalid to me, you cannot validate me. Every day I am alive I will continue to cry out. I am confident *He will* stop for me. I have proven it to be true. My journey started years ago and was guided by God. *He* knew me in my mother's womb *HE ORDERED MY FOOTSTEPS and with JESUS at my side MY LIFE CAME* **FULL CIRCLE**.

(Deuteronomy 28:1-6 & 8) And come to pass, if thou shalt hearken diligently unto the voice of the LORD thy God, to observe and to do all his commandments which I command thee this day, that the LORD thy God will set thee on high above all nations of the earth; And all these blessings shall come on thee, and overtake thee, if thou shalt hearken unto the voice of the LORD thy God; Blessed shalt thou be in the city, and blessed shalt thou be in the field; Blessed shall be the fruit of thy body, and the fruit of thy ground, and the fruit of thy cattle, the increase of thy kine, and the flocks of the sheep; Blessed shall be thy basket and thy store; Blessed shalt thou be when thou comest in, and blessed shalt thou be when thou goest out; The LORD shall command the blessing upon thee in thy storehouses, and all that thou settest thine hand unto; and he shall bless thee in the land which the LORD thy God giveth thee.

PHOTO GALLERY

MTA Retirement

My farewell from the New York City Transit

About the Author

Debbie Duncan was born on the beautiful Island of Trinidad and Tobago. She is the fifth of seven children. Debbie

attended St Thomas Private school which she credits for her firm foundation. She went on to attend Belmont Junior Secondary School and then unto South East Port-of-Spain Senior Comprehensive.

She migrated to the United States in 1987 and resides there to this day with her husband Lennox Whyte. Debbie is a mother and grandmother who enjoys gardening, reading, and studying the Bible. Debbie attended New York City College of Technology and graduated with her bachelor's degree in Human Services. Her hunger and thirst for the knowledge of the Lord led her to pursue her bachelor's degree in Theology. As the scales fell from her eyes and the word of God became clearer, she now understood that before you can wear a crown you must first carry your cross. The adversities, hardships and various beat downs were the path to receiving her crown. Coming out on the other side of her storms solidifies the goodness of God. Following the example of Bartimaeus, one of the blind men mentioned in the Bible, she understood that to be seen and come into the presence of the *Lord* you have to cry out to *Him*. My fellow believers continue to cry out to the Lord, believing that *He* is a rewarder of them who diligently seek *Him*. Awareness of her own frailties and apparent imperfections forced her into submission. Debbie humbled herself and relinquished every aspect of her life to the *Lord*. It was her steadfast and unwavering belief that Jesus died for her and for others like her that brought her to her knees. It was on her knees that Debbie touched *Him,* and she was made whole. Friends the same can be done for you, if you only believe. *Hallelujah.*